LOVE FRIENDSHIP AND THE MAGIC OF THE CAMINO

Lynn Dryden

Dedication

I would like to dedicate this book to Jim, my soul mate forever and beyond; to Tessa, Steven, Rosie and Zoe, love you millions; to my family and friends who are just the best; to Trish my best pal and to all the people I count myself blessed to have met on my Camino.

I would also like to thank Priscilla, my lovely publisher and friend, who is so supportive, positive and patient when I come up with my ideas and who has helped me to get this book out there. It means so much to me and I really appreciate your help and guidance with my writing. Thank you so much.

Published by Brilliant Publications Limited
Unit 10
Sparrow Hall Farm
Edlesborough
Dunstable
Bedfordshire
LU6 2ES, UK

www.brilliantpublications.co.uk

Brilliant Publications is a registered trademark.

Written by Lynn Dryden

© Text, maps and photographs Lynn Dryden 2023
Illustrations Nigel Tinlin
© Design Brilliant Publications 2023

Print ISBN 978-1-78317-353-2

First printed and published in the UK in 2023

CONTENTS

Chapter 1
LOVE

My husband Jim was and will remain the love of my life. We met when we were 17 years old. He was my blind date for an evening out with my best friend and her boyfriend – it was the summer of '69. From the start we just hit it off. He had just started work as a fitter's apprentice. I was in my last year at school. He was easy to talk to, really interesting and he was just Jim. On that first date we found we had so much in common; we chattered on for a couple of hours. He was going off on holiday to the Norfolk Broads the next day with his pals. He said to me at the time he felt sure at least one of them might end up in the water after visiting the pub. I remember saying, "Well make sure it's you who helps to pull them out." He also told me he would get in touch when he got back. He insisted on putting me on my bus that night and gave me a peck on the cheek which I thought was nice.

He did ring me when he came back and that was it, the beginning of Jim and Lynn.

We were married in April 1974, just before I qualified as a teacher. He was doing exams as well so he could become a fitter. Every day we spent together was a blessing. Don't get me wrong. There were some really sad and bad times in our life together, personal tragedies when we lost people we loved; but these tragedies only pushed us closer together and the happy times we had made us appreciate how fortunate we were to have each other.

One of our happiest days, apart from getting married, was the day we had our beautiful daughter. I remember her little red face was wet with my tears of happiness and she was making a right racket, considering how small she was. Jim and I looked at each other and he put his arms around us both and was so proud.

Jim as a dad was one of the best. He adored Tessa and, to her, he was her hero. They were so good together. It was lovely to see him taking her out to play with the other children in our street as soon as she could walk. From being tiny, his heart was hers and, as she grew up, he encouraged her to follow her own heart when it came to making a career choice. He supported her and offered guidance in everything she did and helped make her the lovely person she is today.

He was such a proud Dad and when we became grandparents to Rosie and Zoe it was just like reliving the happy years we had with her. Of course, the girls adored him because he was always fun to be with. He loved Steven his son-in-law and together they always had a laugh and enjoyed the football. Steven, together with our nephew (also called Steven) took him to see the scary German band Rammstein. Jim described their stage act as most unusual, scary and a tad controversial, but he had enjoyed the concert. He was so chuffed that they had asked him to go. He loved being with young people and a good time was had by all. Jim was so loved by all of the family because he was always kind, never judgemental and loved helping people in any way he could.

As a couple we were always there for each other; we were best friends who encouraged each other to develop any new ideas and talents. We helped each other to chase our own dreams and to achieve our goals. Jim studied part time on an evening for his Honours degree and then I did the same. At times we seemed to know what the other was thinking and feeling. If something was upsetting one of us, the other one was upset as well. But we were able to help each other overcome our problems and deal with them so they weren't problems anymore. I remember once I was having a bad time in a school where I only worked for one day a week and, believe it or not, I was being bullied – in my late fifties. Instead of enjoying doing what should have been fun, I dreaded going in because I had obviously been given someone else's job and their nose had been put out of joint. I put up with it for three months and used to moan on about how unfair it was to Jim, but I just kept my head down because I thought if I ignored them they would give up. But everyone knows, unless you sort it, bullies never give up. One day, while I was getting ready to go there, I was moaning on to Jim who had just retired. He smiled at me and just said so calmly, "So how much more are you going to take? What are you going to do about it? What do you tell your kids at school to do? You need to sort it." I looked at him and suddenly I realised what I had to do. I smiled, kissed his cheek and said, "How about I tell them today I'm leaving as soon as I can?" He smiled and all he said, was, "Go tell them babe." So I did. I also told them I wasn't going to tolerate their bullying and unkind behaviour anymore. I was buzzing, I felt so much better, I had handled bullying for my pupils so easily but I needed Jim to make me realise I was a victim myself. He knew how unhappy I was every Friday morning and he could have told me what to do, but he always used to say that sometimes people have to work things out for themselves. So, when he asked what I could do to improve my life, I knew straight away what I had to do; it was so clear. We knew each other's thoughts and could sometimes finish each other's sentences. He was my mentor, he taught me loads about myself. We both had common interests and different interests but we helped each other develop and enjoy them. He liked playing squash, going to the football match, seeing his pals. I liked dancing. We always had time for our hobbies. As we got older and when we retired we developed similar interests. Walking and travelling became our favourite activities. When we bought Ruby our camper van, for the two of us, it was heaven. Our life together once more became as exciting and adventurous like it had been in our very early days together – at heart we were still kids – although our joints reminded us we weren't. We both were really excited by a new life together on the open road. Together we felt we could take on the world. Our love was so strong we could face anything as long as we were together. We had so much happiness together and Jim always used to say, "Life is good and we should never take anything for granted." He was a spiritual person who loved being out among nature and often used to say, "God was so clever when he made the world."

We were all thrown into turmoil when Jim got some test results back that showed he had prostate cancer. He was only 66 years young. He remained positive throughout his treatments. Nothing phased him – he was so brave.

We knew we would all fight together, every step of the way. The two of us – backed up by Tessa, our daughter, Steven, our son-in-law, Rosie and Zoe, our gorgeous granddaughters, the whole family, and our best friends, all of us – were on that journey with him, supporting him, loving him, taking him for treatment, spending precious time with him and hoping and praying for a miracle. But sadly it just wasn't meant to be.

We were all broken hearted when we lost him on January 24th 2018. He had fought bravely for almost three years, with great dignity and we all had loved him through every second of every minute of every single day he was with us. We were all devastated and it was hard to believe he wasn't here anymore.

Jim was and will remain my soul mate. We found each other 50 years ago and we knew in our hearts then that whatever happened to us, we would always be together. And we are still but, being human, I miss seeing his lovely face. I miss holding his hand. I miss him telling me everything is going to be alright. I even miss all the cups of tea he used to make for me. But I know whatever happens to me in life he will give me the courage to get through and I cherish all our beautiful memories together and I know I will love him till the end of time. So I will try to live my life remembering the memories we made and play them like short movies in my mind. I will

cherish them. I will try to be positive and not be drawn to the dark side, as Jim would say. I will count my blessings, having my lovely family on both sides and our friends. I will tell my granddaughters funny stories about him. I will remember how he told me I had to stay strong and keep on keeping on no matter what happens in life, but most of all I will keep him in my heart and soul because I know that's where he will be forever.

One week after losing Jim, I lost my Mam, Joanie, who died in hospital on 8th February. I can't write this book without a word about her. Mam was 87 years old and had lived a good and happy life until dementia kicked in. To us she will always be the best mam in the world, who was happy, fun to be with wherever you went with her. She was famed for her wicked sense of humour which sometimes,  thankfully, became apparent in the worst of situations. Like when she had fallen and broken her shoulder and was admitted to hospital. The specialist unfortunately had such a miserable face and long suffering attitude with her. She asked him what was wrong but when he said, "Mrs Smith you have broken your shoulder", she said "I know that but what's wrong with you? You don't seem very happy." He didn't answer, just grunted, but we were all giggling behind his back. Mam loved her golf and took on important roles in the Golf Club. She was so loved by all of her family and her friends. My Mam was brave and lived her life as best she could without my Dad. But I know she missed him and now I know exactly what it must have been like for her.

Mam was always a sunny, happy person who enjoyed going on holidays abroad. She enjoyed going anywhere with her family – she was game for anything. You could always rely on her support for anything exciting and we will always miss her. But I bet she is playing those golf courses in Heaven with my Dad and catching up with all of her family and relations who she had missed for years. Joanie, we all will love you forever. You were just the best. xxxxxx

Love,

Lynn, Shirley and Peter

Chapter 2
TRUE FRIENDSHIP

Before Jim was diagnosed with prostate cancer we had talked about walking the Camino in Galicia and Jim had said what an adventure that would be because he loved walking. I have to admit, I enjoyed walking with him more than the actual walking itself because Jim was always good to talk to and fun to be with, wherever you were going. He knew the names of all the birds and could tell you which birds made different sounds. He knew loads about the wild flowers and plants. Maybe we should have just decided to walk the Camino as soon as we could but we had just got our camper van, Ruby, and we both were more than happy taking off to some of the most beautiful and more remote parts of Scotland where we were totally surrounded by nature at its wildest and its best. I am so thankful we had our Ruby trips. They are well and truly etched in my mind and on my heart. There is nothing so magical as sitting on a remote beach on Mull, with silver sand and scallop shells gleaming white in the moon light, holding hands with the man you love, head on each other's shoulders watching the moon rise. We must have looked like one of those cute teddy bear pictures you see – but with older looking teddies. Those Ruby trips were so special to us both and we knew at the time we were making special memories. What we didn't know then was how important these memories would become when we were stuck in hospital sometime in the future. We used to say, "Remember when we went to…." There was always something funny to say about everywhere we went together. From the very beginning Ruby was our happy place wherever we went. We both felt the same and we had some really happy fun times. Those memories got us through some really tough times and they help me now when I go away on little trips on my own and with my friends. Ruby is still my happy place.

We held on to the dream of the Camino but soon realised it was slipping further and further out of our reach as the cancer made things more difficult, so we said we would put the trip on hold. We even thought of driving it in Ruby, but all the driving would have been just too much and very uncomfortable for him. So we just shelved the idea and did what trips we could, going away with our family and granddaughters to beautiful places we loved – places where Jim could get treatment fairly quickly if it was needed. Our trips away with our family were golden and it was time well spent which we all will treasure forever. Soon travelling became difficult and almost impossible after Jim suffered a broken hip. It just happened when we were shopping.

After that things just got progressively worse for Jim. We had a wheelchair, crutches and a variety of aids in the house. Jim just carried on business as usual, but I have to say I was a rubbish wheelchair driver. He must have had nerves of steel whenever I took him out. But we went out wherever he wanted to go, his friends and family were there with him every step of the way, taking him out, spending time in hospital with him. We all did what we could. At one point we were finding it really difficult to get him home from hospital, so my niece's husband and all the family helped get him and his wheelchair home in a special taxi. He was so pleased to be home and I can never thank each and every one of them enough for the extra time they gave us at home, where he loved to be. We really enjoyed what time we had with all of our family and loved him so much. Jim never complained once and we all just loved him to pieces for being so brave, so positive and never giving in. The thought of him dying never crossed my mind. I think we both just didn't want to waste what time we had worrying about something we couldn't change. We knew the worst but hope kept us going. Maybe some people would call it blind hope, but I never cried about losing him before it happened because I wanted to live every single second with him like we always did and be able to remember everything. I had loved him for 47 years. I had no idea, and didn't want to know, what I was going to do without him. So I did a Scarlett O'Hara and said to myself, "I can't think about that right now. If I do I'll go crazy." I would worry about it tomorrow.

A few months after Jim died, I thought about the Camino and how Jim had really wanted to walk it. I even wondered if I could do it myself but I kind of convinced myself that I was hardly Camino material. First of all I had lost a lot of weight in the last few months of Jim's life, which I hadn't been aware of. At the best of times, I tip the scales at 7 1/2 stone and that's with my shoes on. I was actually scared to get on the scales, so I didn't. All I knew was that my clothes were baggy and it worried me no end. Then when I saw how skinny I was, I couldn't imagine that I was strong enough mentally or physically to manage it really. So I put the idea of walking the Camino out of my mind. Anyway, the nicer weather was here and my friends went off on Ruby trips with me. My best pal from primary school, Trish, and I went on a trip to Beal near Holy Island and we watched the film, *The Way*. Strangely enough, it was the only film I had in the van at the time. I usually had a stash of DVDs but had left them on the kitchen table. She knew nothing about the Camino till then and I told her it had been an idea to do the Camino with Jim. But I had to say to her that I wasn't a dedicated walker at all. Oh, don't doubt it, I would have followed Jim to the end of the world but I would have slowed him down. He, on the other hand, would have been happy to take his time and wait for me.

Two days later after our trip, Trish rang and asked me if I wanted to walk the last section of the Camino from Sarria to Santiago de Compostela with her. I have no idea why but I just said, "Yes". I didn't even think about it. Then we both panicked that it was too far and we were inexperienced walkers so we decided a few weeks later that our trip was off. But two weeks later it was back on. Trish wanted us to walk it together and get our *Compostela*. She said Jim would be with us, but at that time I had no idea how right she was.

Trish and I have been friends since we were five years old at primary school. We endured life at primary school with a headmistress who was a nun but, I have to say, a nun who made Maleficent look like Tinkerbell. Ask any other pupils who were there at the same time as we were. I bet they got the cane as well – for silly reasons like wearing the wrong colour socks when your school socks were too wet to wear because they had been washed overnight (no tumble driers then) and, you're right, that was me. We were well behaved, "wouldn't say boo to a goose" kids and I still feel sad, as a teacher myself, when I hear other pupils at school at that time, talk about how frightened they were made to feel by her. They still talk about her on Facebook which unfortunately is a sad legacy for anyone. Consequently Trish and I spent most of our time at primary school scared of the cane wielding headmistress whose veil swished and whose rosary beads rattled, as she stormed passed to mete out her own mistaken idea of justice.

Since those days we have always been friends, around for each other when things get tough. Now we are thinking of taking on one of our toughest challenges – the last 115 km of the Camino de Santiago. We are under no illusions about what we will be taking on. We will record everything we do and I intend to write about our preparations necessary for the trip, to help other people out there see that it's possible.

I have read so many books about the Camino in the past. It's hard to believe I am actually going to walk it and then plan to write my own book about the whole journey on the Camino, after completing it. I realise that some of the people who walk the full Camino from St Jean Pied de Port in France, don't like the idea of people like me who only walk the last section from Sarria, getting a *Compostela*. But if you're walking for the right reason, it shouldn't matter. The piece of paper is not why I'm choosing to do it. I want to see if I can actually enjoy every step of the Camino, with my best friend from school who I have known for 62 years and who is always there for me. I want to see if I can understand the love my husband had for nature in all its glory. I want to see if I can feel Jim around me on the Way and I hope to gain the strength which will make me feel more able to cope with my loss and live my life the best I can. What other people think has never been a worry for me and it won't bother me now at all.

Chapter 3
ARE WE REALLY GOING TO DO THIS?

31st May 2019

We booked our flights with Ryan Air through Hays Travel because we wanted the reassurance of having someone else do the booking. We were both capable of booking ourselves. One of Jim's quotes, "Hey how hard can it be?" quickly came to mind, but we just wanted someone else to be responsible. We also booked our trains to and from Stanstead. It looks like we have to make a few changes on the trains, but we have time, so no hassle. We have also booked an open ticket for coming home just in case there are any delays. We need a night at Stanstead so we opted to stay at the Hampstead Hilton for the night which is five minutes away from the terminal – well it looks that way and it's what we were told, so bring it on.

I can't believe I am doing this. I absolutely hate flying and I'm not that fond of walking seriously, but I have to admit the Camino and all its stories has me hooked, excited and just a bit wary. I wonder what type of food I will eat on the Camino because I really am such a plain boring eater. I hate spicy food and would be happy with potatoes and roast chicken any day. My Mam used to say I eat to live, not vice versa, and I will need to put my weight back on and do some serious walking before I can even consider walking 115 km. I know what I have to do and the sooner I start, the better. I feel scared and excited at the same time.

Jim said you always have to keep on keeping on whatever happens in life. In spite of the fact that missing him is the worst feeling ever, I know he would be thrilled that one of my good friends has asked me to walk the Camino and I have actually said yes. I have decided I am going to walk it for him and ask if I can have his name put on the *Compostela*. I realise this might not be possible but I will do my very best to make it happen. It's also a reason to make me walk over hot coals, with a big smile on my face.

Jim loved being outdoors. We both helped with the lambing on my cousin's farm every year. He loved being on the farm and always worked hard. He was a good quad bike driver, flying through the fields with me hanging on tight behind him, on the way to feeding cake (pellets) to the sheep. Sheep love the cake and I was always wary of the way they chased the quad. Jim always laughed when I used to run back to the bike after filling the trough with the pellets. I felt like they were chasing me and would jump behind him and shout "Let's go". He embraced adventures. He walked the Coast to Coast and Hadrian's Wall. He climbed up Creogh Patrick in County Mayo in Ireland. He walked St Cuthbert's Way and was going to start walking St Oswald's Way, to name a few. He loved nature and walking in the fresh air. Now I thought I had better see what it was he liked, because it gave him so much happiness. I hope it makes me feel a bit happier than I do at the minute. I am counting on it.

It's May 2019, We have booked our accommodation in hotels and *albergues* along the Camino through the tour company called Santiago Ways. Our luggage will be transferred daily ahead of us, to our next port of call, wherever we are staying for the night. I'm sure that will annoy any purist pilgrims as well but I really hope that this will work out for us, as I intend having as little as possible in my backpack – just waterproofs and snacks to eat along the Way. I don't feel the need to suffer any more than I already am. Trish and I are no longer spring chickens and the thought of carrying everything we own, as we walk along, for us both, is a non-starter. So, not only are we walking the last part of the Camino, we aren't carrying our 20 kg suitcases either, just our backpacks with whatever we need for the day.

I can't help thinking about one of my heroines, Isabella Lucy Bird, born in Borough Bridge, the fearless famous British explorer, naturalist, writer and photographer who did so many exciting trips on her own. I wonder, did she ever doubt what she was doing or even feel a tad scared? I like to think she may have been, maybe once or twice, but the thoughts of what she was going to see and do gave her the courage to continue her quest. Hopefully by the time we go I might feel more confident, but for now I have to prepare.

I need to buy some comfortable walking shoes then start walking as soon as possible. I need to stop worrying about the fact that I have always hated flying and I have never flown on my own. Usually Jim has always had to lead me on to the plane to my seat, like a high spirited race horse. If I could have been blindfold I would have been happier. I also can be prone to feeling claustrophobic at times on a plane. I have no idea how I will react, but every time we flew I could never sleep the night before. Having said that, my fear of flying has never stopped me going anywhere. I have decided to make my worry list for now:

1. **Not having Jim with me. What will I be like? How will I feel?**
    I have no idea
2. **The transfer to Sarria. Will it be smooth? Will our taxi be waiting? Will my Spanish be up to doing this?**
    I can make sure it is.
3. **Will the hotels and albergues we have booked into be nice?**
    We can always rearrange if they aren't.
4. **Will we be able to walk the distances every day?**
    I can put the work in now so that I am able to.
5. **Will there be food I like?**
    Of course. This is 2019.
6. **Will we finish? Will I get the Compostela in Jim's name?**
    I will do my very best and it won't be for want of trying.

There's way too many things on this list, so it will do for now. All this and the Camino too!

Chapter 4
LOOKS LIKE WE HAVE A GREEN LIGHT

May/June 2019

I don't go until October so the sooner I start walking and eating sensibly to put my weight back on the better. I don't really enjoy eating meat but I will try to eat more chicken as, along with milk, cheese and lentils, it is my only source of protein. My diet is not one of the best as I have mentioned before. I am a very plain eater and tend to eat a high carb diet. I really must focus on my diet as I would like to tip the scales at 7 1/2 or 8 stones by October. But gaining weight when you don't have a big appetite is difficult, so I am drinking milk as well whenever I can. I will try very hard to get stronger than I am at the moment both physically and mentally. I am missing Jim so much but he would be so pleased about the Camino. I just know he is with me at times. I hear his voice in my head helping me when I get so upset and feel so bad. I hope I always hear him, even if I can't touch him or see him. I will be happy to listen to his advice and help whenever I need him. I will think of him like Yoda in Star Wars guiding me.

It's June 2019 and today my friend Trish and I have to check over our booking details. This involves ringing Santiago Ways and making sure everything about our trip is planned. As you can imagine, this is difficult for someone in my present state of mind as there's a hell of a lot of things we need to check over. My main worry is how I will cope solo. It's only been six months since Jim died and I can't begin to describe my feeling of loss. However I have managed to get away for weekends in Ruby, our camper van, and I am so happy that I still get the feeling of excitement I used to get when Jim and I went away together. Ruby was our happy place and she still is. Oh, it's different going with my friends, but I don't feel sad and we have a good time. I am one lucky lady who is blessed with lovely family and friends who are booking themselves in for Ruby trips for the next few weekends. While these trips are different, I do find peace in Ruby. Jim and I had many happy trips in Ruby and I know Ruby will help to heal me in time. I hope I can live my life getting a happy feeling in my heart when I think of all our happy years together and enjoy good times with all the lovely people who are in my life now. I would love to be brave enough to go away on a Ruby trip with my granddaughters on my own at some point in the not too distant future.

I have a lot of work to do to get prepared for the Camino. I really wonder if I can do this but the preparations will focus me and keep me busy, which is what I need. I hope I will be able to walk the distances each day but, more importantly, I really hope I will want to keep on walking.

At the moment, my life is going on and I'm in it but I'm not really, I feel like I'm drifting through time. I really would like this pilgrimage to clear my mind, to give me some peace as well as hope and I want to be thankful for every second of happiness Jim and I had together because in life not everyone is so fortunate.

I feel excited thinking about the times Trish and I will have. What will our friendship on the walk be like? We will always be friends but we have never shared a room with each other for two weeks. Nor have we been in each other's company for 24 hours a day, for 14 days. I say bring it on – I think we will be fine.

Chapter 5
SHOES, SHOES AND MORE SHOES

June 2019

Coco Chanel said, "A woman in good shoes is never ugly." Seo Min Hun said, "Good shoes take you good places" and Marilyn Monroe said "Give a girl the right pair of shoes and she can conquer the world." So you can see that lots of important women and men had an opinion about the right shoes and so the heat is on. Trish and I are going to buy our walking shoes tomorrow. I have a feeling it will be a veritable mare, as the kids say, and of course we will have to consider the socks we will need to wear to keep our feet comfortable. But tomorrow I will need to have an open mind. Jim always used to say when you started anything new "to have an open mind and see what happens".

We visited every shop in Newcastle that sells walking shoes, Trish got her shoes quite quickly but I wasn't quite so lucky. Some of the shoes felt heavier than me and the idea of putting them on everyday filled me with dread. My heels were moving in one pair – that's not good. My toes were hitting the front of the shoe – not good either. Then the assistant brought another pair of shoes out and all that was missing was the white face paint, red nose and a squirty flower and I could have been a recruit for Billy Smart's Circus. If someone had stood on my toes I could have leaned forwards, no problem. So for me, I can safely say, it was not a successful trip. We did manage to get some t-shirts and light fleeces though, to pack in our cases which were now waiting empty in our spare rooms. I really need to get my shoes though, so the next day I became the walk-in nightmare for the poor assistant at Go Outdoors, where to my brother's horror (he was with me), I tried on 14 pairs of walking shoes. Eventually I bought a pair of Merrel Siren Travellers – not waterproof and not what I needed for the Camino – but good for keeping in the van.

So really I still have no shoes for the Camino. It was only when I got home I remembered I had tried on a pair of North Face Hedgehogs, the previous day in Newcastle. I decided to go back, try them on again and, all being well, buy them for the Camino. To me they were the lightest and comfiest shoes I had tried and I needed to get walking. So the next day I went and tried them on with a pair of lightweight merino wool socks. I had to go one full size larger, but they felt great and were black and turquoise. Making sure you have the correct walking socks can make or break your Camino I'm told, so I bought the socks as well. In fact I bought a few pairs, all merino wool.

Well it looks like we are both sorted out for footwear and we have a friend who is coming over to my house tomorrow, who walked 335 km of the Camino. He is coming to give us some tips and to answer any questions or worries we may have. Alan is in his 70s but you would never believe it to look at him and is one remarkable man. We have lots of questions, as we want to ask him about all our preparations, food, gradients, shoes and accommodation.

Chapter 6
A BIT OF REASSURANCE GOES A LONG WAY

Our visit with Alan has really allayed lots of our fears and it has made me feel excited about the trip, but me being me, I also still remain a bit wary – which for me is nothing new. We asked him about the food and he assured us that there is always something that we would like to eat and there are lots of cafés along the route where you can stop for drinks. We talked about everything that worried us and he assured us that if the worst came to the worst and we couldn't walk another step, you could always ring for a taxi to come and help from one of the nearby villages. He said there were posters on some of the trees with

taxi phone numbers on them. He asked us about our jackets. Were they waterproof as it can rain in Galicia? He had walked early summer. We were walking in October so the weather might be changeable. So overall Alan was a great inspiration to us and we were excited when we listened to his tales of how kind the pilgrims you meet on the Camino can be. He told us about how he hurt his back and was laid out flat at the side of the path to ease it. While he was lying, a young man came along asked if he could help him to his *albergue* and picked up his bag and carried it for him, then made sure he was OK.

Trish and I felt excited after listening to Alan. It made us want to get everything sorted in our cases so all we needed to do was concentrate on getting the miles in, walking.

Now it was time to consider the layers we needed to wear. They had to be layers that worked well together so that if it was too hot we would be comfortable and if it was cold we would be warm, but they couldn't be too heavy as our suitcase weight limit was 20 kg.

I always wear layers as I am almost always chilly but I have been reading about merino wool clothing which is lightweight and the fact that it doesn't smell so it can be worn for a longer time without running the risk of being thrown out of places. The idea of being smelly has little appeal. However, if all I can do after walking for 10 miles is lie down, I might change my tune.

It's really funny but I remember learning about merino sheep in geography at school. They thrive in extreme climates, they have almost 360 degree vision which means don't have to turn their heads to look behind them, their hearing is excellent and their wool is soft and fine. I need to check that is correct but that's what our teacher told us years ago and I remembered it. We might even see some on the Camino. I think they must be fascinating creatures. I love sheep, as I have already mentioned, so I will be keeping "an eye open" for them, as we Geordies say. In the shops the assistants assure me that all these layers will keep me warm and cool, even though I find it hard to believe. I err on the side of caution and choose a fleece that's light as a feather but also warm.

In former times the pilgrims who walked to the Finisterre burnt their clothes there, as a symbol of becoming a new person, having completed the Camino. I think if we were to do that we might not be allowed back on the bus. It's now June 14th. I am still walking in my shoes but I have to say they feel very comfortable every time I wear them. They are waiting with my light to medium weight merino wool walking socks for their maiden voyage up what used to be an old pit heap which is now a beautifully landscaped wagon way. How long do you have to walk around the house in shoes to see if you are going to keep them? Walking up and down a slope in the shop is not really like a shale-covered uneven slope but I am listening to the experts and doing everything I am told. So the Hedgehogs go out today on their maiden voyage. Hedgehog report: they did well, still comfy after 10,5000 steps, so I'm feeling positive. We know we will have to walk, train hard and, most of all, be persistent and determined to be able to complete our walk. By putting in the training now, it will help us to achieve our *Compostelas* and that is what we want.

We will definitely keep that in mind.

It's another weekend and I have things planned, which for me is essential or else I would be walking around the house feeling lost, sad and lonely. I enjoy being out with Tessa, Steven and the girls who are like a breath of fresh air. Keeping busy is important to me because it stops my mind going to dark places and remembering times that upset me. I am helping the girls to choose holiday clothes today, which will mean a Nanny's treat. Watching a nine year old and a six year old choose clothes is an education and an experience everyone should enjoy. As for the Hedgehogs, my shoes are in the porch waiting to go on a walk around the Metro centre which is guaranteed to test any shoes, as its hell on the feet ordinarily. Although there aren't any steep hills and muddy paths, there are stairs – lots of them. Well my Hedgehogs had a good workout and so did I. The trip there cost me because granddaughters are always expensive but so worth it, every penny.

I have decided I had better check out the gear I already have for the Camino against the list we have received from the tour company. The fact that we won't be carrying our luggage in our backpack is the best news ever because, if you are carrying a backpack, how do you decide what you are going to take and what you will leave at home? Speaking for myself at this point in time, I really would have no idea.

I have an old Berghaus jacket which I will wash in the waterproofing liquid then respray when it is dry. I always wear this jacket when I help my cousin Pam and her husband Tom with the lambing. The weather in the Borders can be soaking wet at times and even when riding the quad in heavy rain it has never let me down, so it is going with me. I wonder if it looks too shabby but I ask myself, do I really care? In my present state of mind, of course I don't, as long as it keeps me dry and it's light as anything.

Today is a Saturday and I don't really like weekends when I don't have any plans. As a rule I try to get away in Ruby up the coast with one of my friends if the weather is nice. I have to say they have all been great since Jim died and I have plenty of weekends away planned for the Summer. This weekend is a family weekend and we are planning a walk to one of Jim's favourite places: Linhope Spout in the Ingram Valley, Northumberland. So there will be all of my family and nieces and nephews and Jim's brother and his family. We all have our picnics in our backpacks and the weather is beautiful. It was such a nice thing to do and, although we all missed him, everyone was happy and joking on and enjoying the scenery and each other's company. We rounded the day off with drinks all round at a country pub on the way home.

Being with people is good, but when you are left on your own and everyone has gone home my sadness sometimes overwhelms me and I worry how I will get through this awful time in my life. I say get through but it's not getting through at all, it's being able to cope with and accept the way your life is now and try to enjoy it and be as happy as you can. Then I remember how tough Jim had it and how bravely he fought his battle. I know I have no option but to live my best life for Jim, for my family and for me. I wonder how will I feel when I'm walking the Camino? Will I have meltdowns? Will I be sad? How will I cope? I have loved my life with the best husband in the world for almost 48 years. What happens if I get upset? I suppose, after what has happened, shedding a few tears as I'm walking along the Camino is nothing to worry about. These meltdowns pass; it's always silly things that trigger them. Like the other day, I saw a mobility sign in the Metrocentre which made me remember the first time I took Jim there in his wheelchair, which for him must have been a white knuckle ride because my wheelchair pushing skills left a lot to be desired. At the helm I was a danger to anybody and anything that came within a foot of me.

Jim had wanted a new Levi's jacket and the whole expedition was a hoot for us both. First of all, Jim said he was able to propel himself around the counter where the jackets were, shooing me off to buy my favourite perfume not far away. Unfortunately the arm of the wheelchair got jammed under the display table holding the jackets. He just sat quietly, waiting and trapped, till I came looking for him and we just laughed. He was always fun to take out and I always remained a bad wheelchair driver. One weekend we decided we would go for a wheelchair walk at Amble, where there are great views of the sea from the long pier. On a windy day you can even taste the salt. The idea was excellent but Jim was nearly ejected when I hit a kerb I didn't see, before we were even out of the car park. I got such a shock, I started to cry. Jim just held my hand, said he had every faith in me and insisted I push him. I was always very careful watching where we were going after that as he was precious cargo. What I'm saying is, I never know what the trigger will be to make me sad or upset, but I do know for sure in all his pain and suffering, there was still plenty of room for laughs and special happy moments.

I digress, and I just bet you're wondering how the North Face Hedgehogs are doing. Well I'm averaging about 12,000 to 15,000 steps a day and crying pints of tears on a regular basis. My daughter says I should try to relax when I'm in the house instead of finding stuff to do, but the truth is I can't because it's hard getting used to being in on your own. I talk to Jim, ask his advice and, yes, I do get answers that either come into my head or become so clear. I just wish I was more spiritual so that I can accept that he's around me but I keep doubting and I shouldn't. I'm hoping the Camino might give me some answers. For two and a half years I prayed like mad and sometimes there would be an improvement and other times there would be new problems which we had to take on. But, I have to say, we both always had hope and so did the doctors and nurses. Having hope was a great feeling. So I really want to learn how to accept my life now and cope with it and be happy with what I had and with what I have now.

Anyway back to preparations. I have bought some medium grade socks with fingers for each toe. They just cover my ankle and are so comfortable to walk in. I have curly toes and at first I couldn't get my toes in properly but they are brilliant and my feet feel so comfortable. I bought them at a sports shop and the owner, who regularly runs marathons said they were very good socks. He was right. So now the feet are well sorted and the layers are not far from being packed either.

As I said previously, I am usually always cold and I get teased because I could do the Dance of the Seven Veils and still have clothes on. I looked at the climate in Galicia in October and it can vary from high temperatures of 25°C to lower temperatures of 15°C so I have a dilemma. Merino wool is soft and lightweight but is quite expensive, so what do I do? I have gone for ordinary lightweight walking tops that are easily rinsed through and dry quickly, not that I'm planning on doing any washing. I have six tops that I can alternate and a couple of t-shirts as well, to change into when we are relaxing. I have a hot lightweight fleece and two very lightweight fleeces that will go under my jackets. Yes, I have my Berghaus as back up and a new lightweight waterproof jacket which I picked up in Keswick; it called out to me from the hanger "Buy me" and I had no choice but to try it on and get my card out. I spoke to the man and he said I should test the jackets by turning the hosepipe on in the garden and stand under it to see if I got wet. My Berghaus passed the test but I didn't bother with my new one because it was new – maybe I should have. Now I need to consider walking pants. I have some waterproofs I can pull on over walking trousers if I have to and will carry them in my backpack, but have decided to go for shower-proof walking trousers and another pair that are supposed to be very good. I reckon that with my shoes, they could walk to Santiago themselves. I am also putting some lightweight ones in just in case it is, dare I say it, hot. It's the end of June now so things are starting to come together and I'm feeling happy about the walking gear I have got.

Jim had bought himself a new backpack when he walked the Coast to Coast, so that will be the one I will take on the Camino. Just in case it's not waterproof I've bought a cover for it. When I looked inside he had everything I would need for a long walk and I felt a deep feeling of love for him, tinged with real sadness, but also a new determination to do the Walk. I should have been sad, looking at the stuff all neatly packed by his own hands but I heard his voice in my mind saying, "There you go Babe, everything you need is in there, no stress." Jim was so tidy everything was always in the right place. I am sorry to say I am the opposite, or I was, but now I'm trying so hard to keep things in the right place because it makes life so much easier. I think he would be proud because I have actually picked up some of his good habits.

Chapter 7
KEEP YOUR EYES ON THE PRIZE

July 2019

My Hedgehogs are getting the miles in. I'm doing about 16,000 steps easily every other day and I am hoping they will carry me all the way from Sarria to Santiago with the minimum of pain and fuss and, of course, blister free.

This weekend I am heading off to Dunbar on a two day girly Ruby trip with my friend Pat where we plan to do some walking and sightseeing around the town. We walked for five miles around Burns Ness Lighthouse and the surrounding area in Dunbar.

There was a young couple on the beach obviously going through their wedding service with their friends. I hoped that they would be as happy as Jim and I had been and wished them all the best, even though they were too far away for them to hear me. I sat overlooking the beach remembering all our happy times and smiling at the lovely little and big things that Jim would do as a surprise for me. Like when he planted me a beautiful window box which took me two days to notice! When I finally did, he just laughed and said he wondered when I was going to notice it. Like when he hired a super sports car to tour the American south. We drove up Elvis Presley Boulevard in a midnight blue Chrysler Seebring with the top down and checked into the Heartbreak Hotel. Like when he wrote a special song for me for our ruby wedding celebration and sang it to me in front of everyone, playing his guitar with his two friends. Everyone knew how much we loved each other and I do have lots of happy memories, but sometimes I feel like I'm living my own Camino at the minute, waking up to it every day and thinking of different ways to get along it.

I hope that this trip will perk me up enough to deal with more sadness which will be helping my brother and sister to sort out Mam's house because we will need to put it on the market very soon. There's a whole lot going on in my head and I am wondering how I'm coping, but I just have to, for my beautiful family. I wake up and feel desperate, crying into my cereal wondering how the hell I can do things. How can I talk to people, smile and at times even enjoy what I'm doing? I am doing things and I am talking to people and I am even smiling and enjoying myself. But it's coming back home that is hard, sitting on the settee on your own and having meals on your own, even seeing stuff in the freezer that you never eat. Then, after all of this, going to bed on your own after making sure everything is securely locked. I really hope I will get used to this without being sad all of the time.

My Hedgehogs, you will be pleased to hear, are now in Ruby with my merino wool socks ready to take some good terrain in the lakes in the next few days. My friend Marg and I are off to a campsite which is within walking distance of Bowness town centre. You will be pleased to hear that the weather is amazing – a bit too hot for me if I'm honest. We are using our bus passes and travelling all over the lakes as well as taking in a few shops on the way and, of course, walking for miles. We even got interviewed on the bus to Grasmere by a young man from India doing a travel blog. The number of steps is ramping up but I'm not really noticing, which is all good. We walk, then stop for a cuppa, but my friend sometimes prefers a cocktail on the way home. I would say I'm definitely doing my best to walk whenever I can and with whoever wants to come along with me.

Today is the Race for Life which I have done every year with my friend Gill for the last several years or more. I was bothered in case I couldn't face the start of the race which is always emotional for everyone there. I was scared I was going to break down, but we shed our tears then got started. Every year we are congratulated for the money raised by the race and it's all very positive. I just wish that the research could be speeded up so that more people benefit, but I have to say that Jim had every possible treatment available for his cancer. I'm really grateful to all the fantastic nurses and doctors who helped us.

If you read about cancer treatment there is always the hope that there will be a successful treatment in the next few years. I like to think it is more than just hope – hope with the possibility of a positive outcome very soon.

Well as far as our walking gear is concerned, dare I say it, I think I am nearly sorted and so is Trish. My Hedgehogs are well on their way to becoming the soft slippers I hoped they would and I am loving my comfy walking socks. I have started walking with my backpack on with exactly what would be in it were I walking the Camino. I seem to take ages to make my mind up about things and don't get flustered like I used to. I guess they don't seem important to me and I know I will sort them out at some point. I really think I am more chilled out like Jim used to be. Nothing bothered him. He just used to say, "It is what it is, let it happen." So I am trying my best.

Chapter 8
ACCEPTING THIS DIFFERENT LIFE

July 2019

I would like to say a little bit about living on your own. Living without your partner is not easy as you have to have a bit of knowledge about things you never bothered about, especially in the house. Like today, I am getting a new garage door. It's one of those electric ones that rolls up. Obviously the man had to show me how to operate it and what to do if it jammed. My knowledge of electricity is basic but I know where the fusebox is and where my candles are. Apart from that I know very little else and I prefer it that way. Jim's reputation working with electricity was also a bit dubious. One day when they were working together, my brother asked Jim to switch off the supply at the mains. Jim went to do so and shouted it was switched off. The horror of seeing my brother flying across the room, swearing profusely at him was the end to his electrical reputation and a source of amusement in the family. Jim and electrics was a definite no no. So the door is fine. It works and occasionally will need lubricating to stop it making a noise as it rolls up.

As for other work in the house I am limited. I can paint but can't hang wallpaper and, I have to say, the idea of painting a large room wouldn't be something I would really fancy doing myself. I can cut the back garden but with help from John the gardener. However, I cut the front lawn which is quite small. As for digging, the soil in our garden is mostly clay and like bell metal. I can't even get a trowel to penetrate so I rely on my long suffering gardener, John, to dig over the borders. As for things going wrong in the house, like plumbing, heating or conservatory leaks, I am fortunate to know good trade people who have done work for us before and who know me. I can ring them when something goes wrong and I know they will sort things out for me. But not having Jim to discuss things with is awful. Fortunately my son-in-law, daughter and family help me to get things sorted as well.

I wanted to change our car because we had planned to before Jim died. It took me ages to decide what I wanted. Then when I went to the dealers. I had two to see. I have to say, going to look at cars on your own is a bit daunting but I did succeed at looking at them on my own and even asked them some questions. Some garages have ladies to speak to if you want but these days you tend not to get the hard sell. I made my mind up, got a good price on my car and bought a Mini Countryman. I have to say, it is like sitting in the cockpit of an aeroplane – it does everything but fly! I felt happy with my deal and my confidence was really boosted.

I am a great believer in knowing what I want, how I expect to be treated and stating clearly what I do not need. I find when talking about jobs that need doing, the experts listen and the majority will do a good job for you. Being timid is not an option if you want a good job doing in or around the house when a member of your family can't do it. Be polite, be assertive, weigh things up and discuss the price in advance. If you have any doubts, discuss them with your family and find someone else to do the job.

It is a good idea to make a list of the people who have done good jobs for you in the past. My list has on it: a good electrician, a good plumber, plasterer and painter and decorator, a good builder, a good garage to service your car and a good, kind teenager – in my case granddaughters, nieces and nephews – to help with any technology problems you may get with your i-pad, phone or computer. It is good knowing you can call on dependable people to help you in a time of crisis. I was unlucky enough to get a puncture when my friend and I had been away for the weekend in Ruby. But all I did was ring the RAC and they were there within 30 minutes so it wasn't the end of the world. I believe that most people are good and all you have to do is ask for their help when you need it. Jim might not be here with me physically but I know he is helping me along this awful road and trying to make things easier for me.

Chapter 9
DARE WE SAY, "ALMOST READY"

July/August 2019

Our training is going well and we are both ramping up the miles (or kilometres) every day. Trish is walking her dogs and getting the miles in and my training is going well and I feel very happy wearing my Hedgehogs. They have an important job to do and I have every confidence in them. I am happy with the assortment of clothing I have in my suitcase to take away so I am off to a concert tonight at the Sage, Gateshead. It is the Americana Festival and my friend and I are going to see Eve Sellis in concert. Jim and I were real fans of country music and spent time in Nashville, stood on stage at the Grand Ole Opry playing guitars and saw many of our favourite country artists and bands in concert and festivals in the USA and here in the UK. We both started guitar lessons with a friend Nick who plays in a band and I still play. I don't think I'm a natural but I enjoy it. My friend Marg who got our tickets also likes country music so we were excited to be attending the concert. Eve sang so well. Then she started talking about how she had lost someone close very recently and she had written a song about her loss. She sang it with tears rolling down her cheeks and I knew her pain; I knew exactly what she felt. It was all about talking about your loss, remembering the good times and thanking God for all the good times you had with that person – which really makes sense and is great advice – but is very hard to do when you miss them every minute.

Chapter 10
BRING IT ON - WE ARE READY TO GO!
THE JOURNEY TO SANTIAGO

30th September 2019

Steve Jobs said something about the first step being the hardest one. I think this is so apt for our own big adventure because today is the day we set off on our journey. We have been preparing for months and now we have to hope that all our preparation will pay off. My brother took us to the station with our heavy cases and our backpacks in the boot. I felt like a little scared kid standing waving to him as he drove away, leaving us with our cases. The impact of what we were going to do really hit home. It is plain to us both that suitcases weighing 20kgs are way too big and heavy for two lightweights like us. They pulled us down the slope on to the platform in Newcastle Central station. We were like Marty McFly on his hoverboard in *Back to the Future*, except we were on suitcases. Waiting on the platform was a bit scary, wondering if we would be able to lift our cases up on to the train. We managed to get them on to the new Azumar train but there was no space so we had a struggle to pile them on two seats that people had started using for luggage storage. The ticket lady said that in future people would only be allowed to carry a small amount of luggage. It was the same story from Peterborough to Stanstead – a total lack of space. We have only brought stuff we need and are struggling physically to cope with it. My case has been sorted, packed, unpacked and packed again. I have been in and out of it looking for stuff that was never in there in the first place but in my backpack. It's actually like a reflection of my head – at times in one hell of a muddle.

My pal Trish is good company and has happy memories of Jim so it is great to be with her. I am sitting in our room at the Hampstead Hilton. We have had our evening meal and are watching Jamie Oliver cooking spaghetti on TV. Trish is the cook. I am reading my book thinking maybe could take up cooking in the future but I doubt it. We checked our tickets for tomorrow and we are ready to go, lights out and excited thinking about tomorrow.

1st October 2019

The first challenge for me today was getting into a lift to get into the airport. Did I tell you I hate lifts? Because of the cases we had no option. I get claustrophobic but it was fast and I was pleased to get out. My bag was taken to one side because I had hand washing liquid in a small bottle but then we boarded the plane. We couldn't believe we were on our way and we soon arrived in Santiago.

I had stayed in Santiago in 1998 when I attended a two-week Spanish language course at the university. Because it was Valentine's Day when I was there, Jim had arranged for a bouquet of flowers to be delivered to my room. How he managed such a feat when there was so little English poken amazed me because it took me hours to actually get a vase elivered to my room. This was due to the fact my Spanish was so basic nd also due to not knowing my numbers past 50 at the time. But it was o typical of Jim and made me so happy when I was a bit homesick.

Today though we were met at the airport by our taxi driver, José, olding up a board with our names on, first time ever. I had exhausted ly Spanish an hour into the journey but we found out José supported he "Toon" so we talked about football and all our favourite footballers in oth languages all the way to Sarria.

CREDENCIAL
DEL PEREGRINO

CATEDRAL DE SANTIAGO

Got Sanctiagu.
¡E ultreia! ¡E suseia!
Deus adiuva nos

Codex Calixtinus *Dum pater familias*
[f. 222 (193)] De Sancto Iacobo

El Sepulcro del
Apóstol, meta de la
Peregrinación Jacobea

Chapter 11
THIS CAMINO IS FOR REAL

Arriving in Sarria
Tuesday 1st October 2019

I had read up about Sarria in advance of our visit. Apparently it's famous for antique fairs, has two lovely churches – the Iglesia San Salvador and the Iglesia Santa Maria de Sarria – and has areas of natural beauty down by the river. There was also a lovely shoe shop near our hotel which was so very hard for me to ignore and resist but I couldn't have squeezed another pair of shoes into my case. It's also the place people leave from to take in the last section of the Camino. When we arrived mid-afternoon it was rather hot and sunny, a bit too hot for me.

Our hotel was fine, if not a bit basic. I think we are pilgrims who at this point in time like a bit more luxury but, hey, we can do basic. However the hotel didn't serve food till after 9pm, so we went out to do a reccy to see if we could find somewhere to eat as it was nearing 6pm and we hadn't eaten since lunch time and that was a sandwich in the taxi. We found a little restaurant and had burger and chips. It was hard to ignore the fact that more and more people were coming into the restaurant to watch a football match between Real Madrid and Club Brugge. Seeing Zinedine Zidane reminded me of Jim, who would have known the names of all the good players. He would joke on with me and

ask me who they were. I used to make up names and he would pretend he was training me for Mastermind – just a silly game we played. But I have to say, whenever we did a real quiz I often could name the footballer. Years earlier he had recognised a famous player in Seattle fish market. I think his surname could have been Alvarez but wouldn't swear to it. Jim had a conversation with him and his teammates when we were in the fish market with fish flying past us. This memory made me realise how much I was missing Jim, but it had made me decide that walking for Jim would be the best motivation in the world to keep me going. Trish and I watched some of the match but were tired after our long journey so decided to go back to our room and sort out our stuff for the walk tomorrow. I'm 100% certain tomorrow will be a big shock to the system. Maybe not for Trish but for me it's a certainty or, as Jim would say, "a knocking bet".

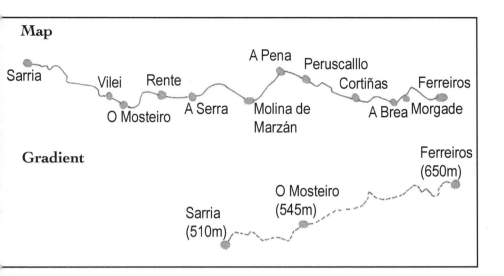

Map

Sarria · Vilei · Rente · O Mosteiro · A Serra · A Pena · Molina de Marzán · Peruscalllo · Cortiñas · A Brea · Morgade · Ferreiros

Gradient

Ferreiros (650m)

O Mosteiro (545m)

Sarria (510m)

Sarria to Ferreiros

12.9 km or 8 miles

Wednesday 2nd October 2019

At breakfast we spoke to a couple who said they would show us how to get to the start of the Camino. To get to the start we had to walk up what seemed like a very steep street with hundreds of steps, I exaggerate of course because my feet, legs and hips were pleading for mercy but we kept going.

We had our Camino passports and we knew we had to get stamps wherever we went. We got our first stamp from our hotel. We were leaving Sarria headed for Ferreiros, a parish which had got its name from the blacksmiths who lived in the area and who repaired the shoes of the pilgrims and, of course, horse shoes throughout history. It is also the place where you can see the 100km marker to Santiago. We were excited and a bit worried about how we would cope with the route. It was about 13km and wasn't particularly difficult people said.

We had made our own sandwiches in our hotel room and had a drink in our backpacks, but we knew we would be stopping on the way at some point just for a cuppa or a loo break.

The walk was quiet and a lovely little robin flew on to a branch right in front of us. It didn't fly away as we approached. Other people saw it and commented on it as well. Then Trish said it might be Jim keeping an eye on us and we both laughed. We walked through woods, through lovely little villages. At one point we had to walk across an open railway line under the viaduct of the Lugo-Monforte road – that was early on in our walk just after leaving Sarria. The first villages we reached were Vilei, C Mosteiro then Rente, A Serra, Molino de Marzán, A Pena, Peruscallo Cortiñas, A Brea, Morgade and then, later in the afternoon, Ferreiros where we were staying for the night. En route we had met and talked to so many people who I'm sure we will keep bumping into on our way to Santiago. We stopped at a café and talked to two ladies called Pat and Mickey from Minnesota and Montana who were great friends and so enthusiastic about the Camino. We said we would see them later that day at the albergue.

We had booked a private room in the Casa Cruceiro De Ferreiros which was all there was really, at Ferreiros. We arrived there about 3:30pm, having enjoyed our walk and our talks. Our bags had been safely delivered to our room which we were pleased about. I think whoever had decorated our bedroom must have loved purple, but the beds were really comfortable. After a shower we decided to order food as we were hungry instead of eating late. I ordered boiled potatoes with grated cheese, as near to a jacket potato as possible. I have already told you that I am a very plain eater and hate spicy food so I won't be regaling you with tales of cuisine. I eat to live. I did get some funny looks from people but I didn't care.

The sun was still shining so we explored our surroundings and opted or an early night because we planned an early start the next morning. At home I'm a night owl but here I was sharing a room with Trish who njoys an early night. I had a torch so I read my book till 10pm, then was ready to sleep. I thought about the scenery we had seen today: he views were breath taking and the gradients were amazingly breath aking, in places. At the moment my legs and hips are in the dark about omorrow's walk so I will keep it that way for now. Night! Night!

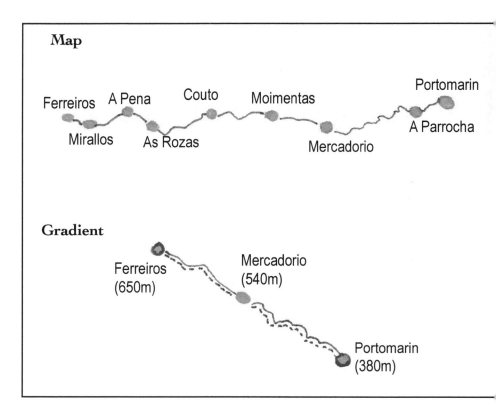

Map

Ferreiros · A Pena · Couto · Moimentas · Portomarin
Mirallos · As Rozas · Mercadorio · A Parrocha

Gradient

Ferreiros (650m) · Mercadorio (540m) · Portomarin (380m)

Ferreiros to Portomarin
9.1 km or 5.6 miles
Thursday 3rd October 2019

I slept so well last night and woke up to Trish's alarm, at 6:30am. It was still very dark when we got up and went over to the bar for our breakfast which was toast and *mermelada* with tea. I really missed my cereal but thank goodness we had brought a stash of food with us to munch along the route to Portomarin. This is the town that was moved in 1960 when the river Mino was dammed and the Belesar reservoir came into being. The old village was flooded but the 12th century Romanesque churches San Xoan de Portomarin and Capelo de San Pedro, were moved piece by piece. In summer, when the water level is low, you can see some of the old village especially the old Roman Bridge just beside the modern day bridge, so we were looking forward to seeing this.

We set off walking in starlight. As long as I live I will never forget the magic and beauty of the early morning sky. The stars were still twinkling and the sun was just starting to come up, adding a pink glow to the sky. I took a photo with my phone but it didn't do it justice at all. We walked on our own for about an hour then we met a lady called Tina who had travelled from Phoenix in Arizona who wanted to tell us why she was walking the Camino.

Tina's story was very sad. Her only daughter, who was her best friend and who always went on trips with her, had died in a horrific car accident and she wanted St James and her daughter to somehow let her know that there is a Heaven and that she was at peace in Heaven. Tina had no doubts at all that her request would be granted and her faith was amazing and, at the same time, very moving. She was carrying everything she had with her on her back. When we arrived at an extremely steep stony part of the route we all helped each other down what appeared to be a dried out waterfall which was very steep and a bit dangerous. It was a bit stressful but we made it down by throwing the bags first, then making our way down a level at a time and helping each other. We weren't far away from the town and looking down towards the bridge into Portomarin we could see the old town buildings under the water where the river level was low. The sun was shining and we were so pleased to arrive where we would be staying for the night. It was an amazing sight to see. Unfortunately for Trish, there were gaps between the planks on the bridge and we could see the river below us. She had great trouble walking across because she was panicking, but I told her not to look down and just concentrate on my backpack as I walked in front of her which she was able to do. We eventually crossed the bridge only to be confronted by 40 or 50 very steep stairs which we had to walk up to get into town. Wow! Our lungs were bursting when we reached the top, well mine were. We took photos and sat on one of the few seats at the top where we chatted a bit more and exchanged addresses with Tina. She then went on her way as she had another 15 kms to walk. We said we really hoped to meet up with her again maybe in Santiago, as she was hoping to get to there a day or two ahead of us. We felt a bit sad leaving Tina but we had met so many lovely people and we lived in the hope that we would bump into them again along the Way.

Our hotel, the Vistalegre, was a white modern building in the centre of town. It was well maintained and welcoming. The hotel had spa facilities, a dining room and modern cocktail bar. Our room was very nice, spotlessly clean and it was close to all amenities. It was here I realised that I had left Jim's sun hat, which I had brought on the Camino with me, at our last albergue. The hotel staff rang for me but someone there must have just thought I had left it because I didn't need it – a common practice among pilgrims. I was so upset because it had been his and I had lost it. Poor Trish had to witness a major melt down where I sobbed for ages but eventually saw sense and off we went to the pilgrim's mass in the local church at 6:30pm. It was here I knew my family in Heaven were close to me because the hymn sung solo in Spanish at communion was one of my Nanny and Grandad's favourite hymns: "Nearer my God to Thee". I found this amazingly comforting and enjoyed the rest of the night. After a cuppa for me and a big gin and tonic for Trish we went back to our room to scare the living daylights out of ourselves looking at the gradient for tomorrow's walk. We were walking to Ventas de Narón. After deciding what time we wanted to leave we turned in for the night and opted for a lie in till 7am. In the morning we were so pleased when we saw the breakfast laid out in all its glory: cereals, porridge, eggs bacon – think of anything you want for your breakfast and it was there for you. It was the first decent breakfast we had had. I asked could they possibly put a cheese sandwich up for us to take for our lunch. They were happy to do so for free and asked if there was anything else we needed, which was so kind of them. We said our goodbyes and thanked the staff for their kindness and joined a lot of other pilgrims all walking in the same direction.

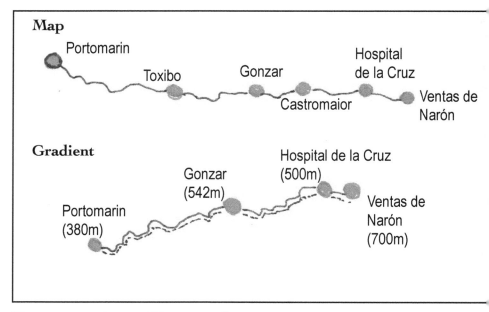

Map
Portomarin
Toxibo
Gonzar
Castromaior
Hospital de la Cruz
Ventas de Narón

Gradient
Portomarin (380m)
Gonzar (542m)
Hospital de la Cruz (500m)
Ventas de Narón (700m)

Portomarin to Ventas de Narón
11.5 km or 7 miles
Friday 4th October 2019

Yesterday had been sunny but today it was dull and a bit damp. At first when we set off, we saw lots of people all going the same way as us. It was a bit like walking out of a football match, with people all around you heading in the same direction. The sound of sticks and walking poles was deafening. Experience taught us that the "crowd thing" happens every day but within 10 to 15 minutes everyone is off on their own Camino and you are left alone. After that you sometimes see them along the road having a coffee.

I had read our notes last night to find that our albergue was all that there was in Ventas de Narón, although there was a tiny chapel beside the albergue which was closed. However in the year 820 this place had been the site of an important battle between Muslim and Christian forces. The

Christians led by King Alfonso 2nd repelled the Muslims, stopping them from expanding their territory to the north. We had opted to have a rest day there as well so we were booked for two nights. We were looking forward to having a break from walking as our legs were aching a bit. We set off at 8:30am. It was a real uphill struggle for quite some time. There was the occasional shout of *velo* which meant we had to jump out the way of a bike or bikes. Usually they were in groups and were not keen to slow down. We walked through Toxibo where we saw a granary or *horreo* at the road side, one of many along the Camino, and had a coffee at a café in Gonzar. The weather got brighter as we approached Castromaior. After that we had quite a steep climb, then passed Hospital de la Cruz, which was a pleasant sight as we knew our albergue was 1.5km from there.

When we got to our albergue it looked very nice and was right next to the tiniest church I had ever seen. We went to our room which was very clean, but we both felt it was a tad rustic and lacked any signs of luxury. However, we are on a pilgrimage so we accepted our lot. Then I went into the bathroom and found there were no lights around the mirror because the bulbs were missing. The room felt cold and was facing the wrong direction to get any heat from the sun at any

time of day. Trish was tired an got into bed with her clothes o because it was too chilly to li on the top and fell asleep. Late on we changed our minds abou staying there for two night We rang the company we ha booked with and told them w were a little disappointed wit the lack of heat and preferre a little more comfort. Th albergue itself was fine and a the staff were lovely as wa the breakfast. We also aske the company to book us into comfortable hotel in the ne town, Palas de Rei, where we had decided we would now be spending tw nights. We were already booked there for one night but, if we were goin to walk tomorrow, we would need them to book us a room for tomorro night. Our hotel in Palas de Rei had no rooms available but they wer able to book us a room in a different hotel. This meant we would hav to move to our original hotel for our second night in Palas, but we didn consider that to be a problem. That night in Ventas we met up with ou American friends, Mickey and Pat, had our meal together and arrange to meet outside the Cathedral on the Saturday night at 7pm, Camin allowing. We all chatted with the other pilgrims then went to bed. Fo the first time, I actually couldn't sleep because I was chilly so I had to pu some extra layers on while Trish was out for the count.

I checked up on the information for tomorrow and discovered that Palas de Rei is 68 km away from Santiago we were getting closer. Yeah! "Palas de Rei" means "palace of the king" – the king at that time being Witiza, the last Visigoth king to reign in Spain and Galicia. It is said that throughout history Galician nobility liked to live here. Thinking about this I fell asleep.

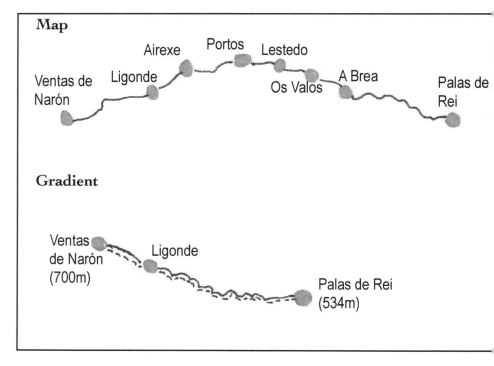

Map

Ventas de Narón • Ligonde • Airexe • Portos • Lestedo • Os Valos • A Brea • Palas de Rei

Gradient

Ventas de Narón (700m) • Ligonde • Palas de Rei (534m)

Ventas de Narón to Palas de Rei

11.8 km or just over 7 miles
Saturday 5th October and Sunday 6th October 2019

We had a good breakfast, made up our sandwiches, snacks and drinks, left our luggage to be picked up and set off at 8am. Trish and I never have a problem getting up early and we are thoroughly enjoying spending time together. For me it's a real treat having her company. We have 12 kms (7 miles) to walk today through lovely little towns and villages Previsa, Lameiros, and Ligonde which are mentioned in pilgrim guides dating back to the 10th century and a pilgrim cemetery. We stopped in Airexe for a cuppa then walked on to Portos (Lestedo), munching our sarnies as we were walking along. Sometimes we would perch on a wall to take in the beautiful scenery as we walked through Os Valos and A Brea, O Rosario and then into Palas del Rei.

I keep mentioning the scenery and today I have to admit to seeing eucalyptus trees for the first time today – they are beautiful. I also saw my little robin early on sitting on a fence. We arrived in Palas de Rei in the afternoon and came across our Albergue San Marco as we walked into town. It looked very nice and the lady  on reception was lovely. We were staying in an annex which was about a ten minute walk through the town. The rooms seemed very modern but the first room we entered was too much like a shop window on ground level; people walking past would easily be able to see in. To say it was minimalist would be kind, so we asked for a room on a higher floor. Changing rooms was not a problem and the second room, while very modern was much nicer and much more comfortable, Once settled we decided to shop for our snacks in a supermarket in town and have a bit of an explore as it was a lovely sunny late afternoon.

I wish I could rewind. We had decided to go to see the famous Concello Square about a ten minute walk away. We indeed got there and were waiting to cross over the road at the town hall when I tripped over a stone bollard which someone had moved out of place and which I didn't see. I fell backwards onto the pavement and felt a terrible pain in my left arm. I managed to get onto my feet with Trish's help but I was badly shaken. We went into a chemist nearby where he looked at my arm, said it was fine and gave me Voltarol. To be honest and very impolite, I might as well have rubbed that cream on my backside. I knew when we were walking my arm wasn't right so we bought some ice and went back to our room. I couldn't move it and the pain was bad so we went to see a doctor in town. She just looked at it and said it was broken and that I needed to go to hospital, 45 miles away in Lugo. I was so worried about it preventing me from walking the Camino and felt gutted. We left the doctor and asked where we could get a taxi. We rang a firm and were told the taxi would be there in five minutes.

We got the crabbiest taxi driver in Palas De Rei, or maybe on the whole Camino, who didn't speak any English and who really didn't want to take us to hospital, in spite of charging us about £50 one way. I tried asking him if he would wait for us and offered to pay him in advance, but no deal. So he dropped us off and left, although he did ask the nurse how long I was likely to be before leaving. We were both shocked, sitting in our cubicle in casualty. In my head I was desperately trying to work out how to tell the doctor everything in Spanish as Trish's Spanish is more limited than mine. You can imagine my relief when he came in and he was an American from California – what a relief! We were both so pleased.

The x-ray showed my arm was broken and that I would need a half plaster. I was told I could continue my walk carefully and fly home without any problems. It was about 2:45am when I was good to go. The man on admissions kindly called us a taxi as both our phones had died hours ago and escorted us outside to the waiting taxi, which I thought was really kind. It was just after 4am when we arrived back at our hotel and the shock of what had happened was kicking in for us both. Trish had

been a great help to me and was going to have to help me with buttons etc until I worked out how to do things myself. We were both shattered and started getting ready for bed but I soon realised I was unable to undo the button on my jeans and felt awful asking Trish to undo my jeans for me. We laughed about her not signing up o be my carer but we managed and eventually I fell asleep with my arm omewhere above my head on a pillow.

The next morning we knew we had to move to our booked hotel. It vasn't far but it wasn't easy with one arm so we just took our time. Getting ur cases down three floors was a massive deal for Trish as they didn't ave a lift for people – only a lift for luggage which was like one of those umb waiters they use for food. So poor Trish was running up and down hree flights of stairs because she wouldn't let me help pull the cases out. Vhen we got to our new hotel we realised it was beside a beautiful church o once we'd left our cases, we visited the church. We found Mass was n so we stayed. My plaster caused a bit of attention. One lady insisted n asking the priest to bless me and our journey on the Camino, which vas very kind but the attention was a bit embarrassing. We coped and ery warily we went out to explore the town. I say warily because my tomach was acting up. It must be the stress of last night. I am relying on mmodium working its magic today and being very careful to eat as bland diet as I can. One good thing about the Camino is you can always get a up of tea. Trish and I sat down to chill out in the sunshine then wander bit more, then decided to sit inside a coffee shop where we were joined y a German lady called Christa who worked as a trauma nurse. She was rom Frankfurt and a kinder, gentler soul you couldn't meet. She said she ad noticed my broken arm in the Church and wanted to wish us a *Buen Camino* and just have a chat. The people you meet are so kind and always ave something very important to say to you. That's what they say about he Camino – it is special and it has lessons to teach us all.

Tomorrow we are walking to Melide. It's about 10 miles and I'm oping my stomach will have settled by then because the thoughts of nanaging the trots in a field or hedge, with my left arm in a plaster and sling, with buttons and zips to undo, not to mention the stiffness in my

calves and thighs from the fall and walking, fills me with terror mor
than the gradients do. The sight would fill other people walking by wit
horror as well, so I'm afraid I might need to test the potency of Immodiu
tomorrow, but I'm hoping I won't. I bet Trish is desperately hoping
works because I can't do zips and buttons yet on my own, it hurts my ar
too much. Too much information!

Trish and I have decided to get up at 6:30am tomorrow, have breakfa
then take off very carefully, as soon as it's light. I would hate another fal
I look at the notes the tour company gave us (as I do every night) to se
what it says about Melide. It's where we will find the oldest Cruceir
on the Camino dating back to the 14th Century, situated in the tow
centre beside the chapel of San Roque. Two Camino routes meet her
the Camino Primitivo and the Camino Frances. From here the two route

become one all the way
to Santiago so it must be
well equipped to deal with
pilgrims. Melide is famous
for cooking an octopus
dish called *Pulpo a Feira*,
boiled octopus, served
best with bread, boiled
potatoes and Ribeiro
wine. I have to say I know
nothing about wines as I
don't drink alcohol but
I reckon if they mention
it specially, it must be
good. Not being too fond
of seafood in general, I
have to say – speaking for

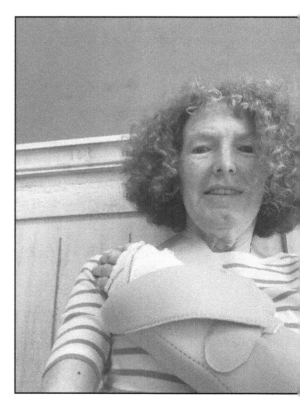

myself – it is not something I would relish unless I had a blindfold on. For me it would be like a bush tucker trial. I have no taste when it comes to food. I am a plain foodie at heart. No offence meant to all octopus gourmets at all, I'm told it's delicious and, if that is what people say, who am I to doubt them.

Melide is also famous for *melindres* (sugar-topped pastries), *amendoados* (almond cakes) and *ricos* (butter based pastries) all of which are made in the town. We were told this by one of the pilgrims we walked with on the way into town. Fortunately, we might need some calories when we get to Melide, as it looks like the gradients are up and down today.

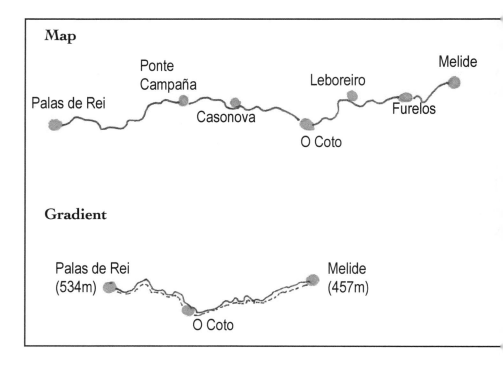

Map

Palas de Rei · Ponte Campaña · Casonova · O Coto · Leboreiro · Furelos · Melide

Gradient

Palas de Rei (534m) · O Coto · Melide (457m)

Palas de Rei to Melide
14.4 km or 8.9 miles
Monday 7th October 2019

Breakfast in our hotel this morning was good. There was a great choice of cereals, fruit, bacon and cooked meats, eggs (fried and hard boiled), croissants, bread, toast – really there was something for everyone with hot and cold drinks. We had packed our snacks and drinks for our walk and were ready to leave. We set off walking through forests of chestnut trees, oak trees and loads of other trees whose names I didn't know but Jim would have. I saw my robin early on in the day and knew Jim was keeping an eye on us as we passed through lovely places like San Xulian de Camino crossing over the Pambre river to Ponte Campaña, through Casanova to O Coto, where we stopped for a drink. Having my plaster on was soooo embarrassing and I got so much sympathy but I kindly accepted all the good wishes. Towards the last 5 km through Leboreiro the route became steeper and there wasn't much shelter. I was worried the heat would get to us both but we were almost in town and we just needed to find where we were staying. I say just find, it was in the centre of town but a long way into the centre. When we got there we were relieved, as always, when we walked into our hotel and saw our cases waiting for us, like long lost friends. They had had an easier journey than us, today. We saw our American pals and walked some distance with them. Then, because we're having another rest day, they will be two days ahead so we won't see them anymore until Santiago now.

We decided to eat here where we are staying, at the Pousada Chiquitin tonight, rather than wait till 9pm. We sat on the terrace and ordered steak with *patatas fritas*. While we were sitting eating, all of Jim's favourite songs came on. I was amazed: he is so here with me and I bet he is loving every minute. You may think I'm mad but I don't care. I bet the vast majority of people who have loved and lost the love of their life will know exactly what I mean. A little robin has been hopping in front of us every day on the Camino and has been sitting waiting for us on the marker stones with yellow marker arrows on. That is no coincidence either. I didn't know, but a visit by a robin is a sign that a lost relative is visiting you. In the spiritual world robins are viewed as a symbol of visits from our deceased loved ones. Robins also symbolise new beginnings and life and are looked upon by many people as a sign of fortune and good luck. I know whatever happens in my life, and wherever I go, Jim will always be with me. I have no idea how I know this but I truly believe it. As Faith Hill sings," Everywhere I am there you'll be." A lady I was walking with today from New Zealand told me the

robin could be Jim or a Tui, a little spirit sent by him to watch over me. I like the idea of the robin being Jim. Our room here in town is nice and cosy so we had a mooch (a Geordie word for look) around town and went into the churches people recommended which were beautiful. Then we went back to plan for tomorrow.

Next stop is Arzúa, 39 km from Santiago. It is a pilgrim town and there is the story about the Pilgrim and the Bread. A poor, hungry pilgrim saw a lady was baking bread in a big oven and stopped to ask for some bread. She said he could have some but would have to pay for it so he left with nothing to eat. He walked on and came upon another house where he saw a lady was baking bread so he knocked on the door. The lady who answered asked him to come into the house to rest and tell him he could certainly have some bread but it wasn't quite ready. The pilgrim insisted he had to keep walking. She was upset and told him she would give him some bread from yesterday. She went to get the bread but when she came back, he had disappeared. She went out on the road to look for him but couldn't find him. When the bread was ready she opened the oven to find the bread had been changed to gold. The opposite happened to the first lady. When she opened the oven it, was filled with stones. Legend has it that it was Santiago himself who had visited both houses. The moral of the story is that whoever helps selflessly is good while greed is never accompanied by anything good.

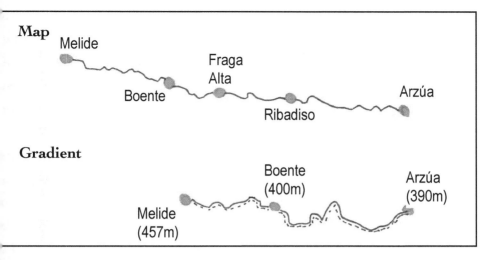

Melide to Arzúa

4.1 km or 8.7 miles

Tuesday 8th October and a rest day Wednesday 9th October 2019

Our breakfast this morning was very continental but there was a choice of cereals so we enjoyed what we had, packed our bags and snacks and set off. We set off in the dark in totally the wrong direction. Thankfully a pilgrim walking behind us gave us a shout and put us right. The weather today is damp and drizzly. As we were walking uphill the drizzle turned to rain and got heavier as the climbs got steeper. The route is very up and downy today, with steep sections up and down roads, through trees, on tracks – a bit of every kind of terrain. Heavy rain is not fun to walk in, especially when you find your new jacket is not as waterproof as you thought. Trish and I have both donned our waterproof trousers. Our walking shoes are fine but my plaster is getting wet through my coat sleeve. The doctor told me not to get my plaster wet so I have taken my arm out of my coat sleeve and it's inside my jacket. Then I realised it was too dangerous walking like that so had to try to keep it out of the rain as best I could. There was no time to stop for a coffee this morning because it was wet and raining and not many indoor seats so we kept going. It seems to be all uphill and it's tough. Eventually we spot a sign for Arzúa and see the steep gradual rise of the road into town. It was peeing down and we were wet. I was walking in front of Trish and when I turned around I could see she was struggling. The incline was so long and steep into town and the rain was running down our faces. I was struggling too so I waited for Trish and we walked together. We were thrilled when we saw a café at the top of the hill. We had instructions to ring our next hotel when we arrived in Arzúa. We walked into the café and the lady took one look at both of us dripping water all over her floor and brought us two teas and some cake without even asking. We were so pleased to be there and that tea tasted like the "nectar of the gods", as my Dad used to say. The walk today had pushed us both to our limits because it had been long, on the steep side and we had walked in heavy rain for a good few hours. We both sat silent getting our breath back, wiping the rain from our faces as we pushed back our dripping hoods. Then we grabbed our cups chinked them together and both said, *Salud*. We rang our hotel and they came to pick us up. The man kindly waited for us as we finished our tea and cake.

We were staying at the Casa Branderix which at first glance seemed more to Trish's taste then mine. It is a 15th century farmhouse. Our room is a kind of annex with a massive wooden door. It reminds me of the entrance to a hobbit house. Inside there are two massive beds, two showers, two toilets and two wash basins in a side room and something that I hope is a heater because the room has a stone floor. I do hope I'm wrong but I have a feeling it might

get chilly in here tonight. Unfortunately, my plaster limits the layers I can wear. Because most of my fleeces go over my head which is almost impossible, I need a zip front fleece or sweatshirt. I was able to buy one so I guess it will be well worn when I get home. There were quite a few pilgrims staying here tonight. We chatted to three American men from New York who were doing the Camino together. Then we met a couple from Toronto who were walking with their friend who had recently lost his wife. We met a really lovely lady called Ann from Ireland who like me had just lost her husband. We are still in touch with each other. The meal that night was very nice and we were hungry. Everyone you meet has a story to tell and each one is special – everyone is seeking something or hoping for the Camino to help them.

Well I was wrong about being cold that night as there was underfloor heating so we were snug as bugs — two very tired ones. Breakfast was once again continental but there was cereal, bread, jam, croissants, *jamon* — really something for everyone. We have a rest day here so we popped into the nearest town because I needed a support sling for my arm which I got at the *pharmacia*, had a walk around some interesting shoe shops which was torture. I say "interesting" because why is it you always see shoes you like when there is absolutely no chance of fitting them in your suitcase?

There was a beautiful Church we had to visit, then we jumped into a taxi to go back to our hotel. The taxi driver was so nice and friendly and our Spanish was much improved by the time we left the car.

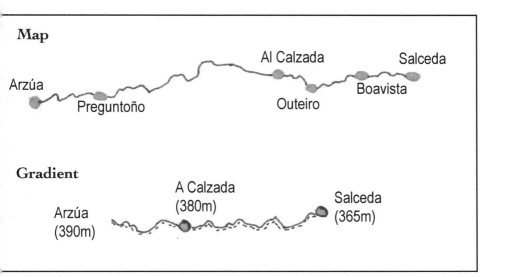

Map

Arzúa · Preguntoño · Al Calzada · Outeiro · Boavista · Salceda

Gradient

Arzúa (390m) · A Calzada (380m) · Salceda (365m)

Arzúa to Salceda

11.3 km or 7 miles

Thursday 10th October 2019

Today we were walking to Salceda, about 11.5 km. The gradient looked good, not too steep. We would be walking on wooded trails, through forests of oak and chestnut trees and prairies – well that's what our notes told us. We had never walked across a prairie and we wondered if they were bigger than our fields here in England. They turned out to be just big fields – nothing to get excited about really. We passed through Preguntoño on to Peroxa, As Quintas, A Calzada, Boente and Boavista, always managing to get a cuppa and a break or meal on the route. We finally reached our accommodation for the evening, the Pension Albergue Alborada, set just off the N-547. When we arrived our suitcases were waiting but there were two flights of stairs for Trish to negotiate with two 20kg cases. The stairs were steep and Trish really struggled but she managed. How I have no idea as I only had one arm and I was neither use nor ornament. We both realised she would never be able to take the cases down so I went to ask the lady on the desk if someone could help us the next morning and she said she was unable to help. I went back to our room and phoned our tour company and explained the situation. They said they would tell the driver who picked up our cases to get them from our room. Our room was as chilly as the reception we had received from the young girl on the desk. There was no heating on and not many blankets so I asked if the heating would be coming on. The lady on reception waved her arms around, very annoyed and said there was *nada* (nothing) she could do. So when I asked, could we have a couple of blankets till it came on please, you can imagine she wasn't a happy bunny at all. Eventually the heating did come on and they brought us two blankets, but I have to say it wasn't really the welcome we were expecting. The staff we dealt with were grumpy and did very little to help. It was disappointing because everywhere else we had stayed the people were lovely and so kind and pleasant to talk to. Fortunately, we didn't have to eat breakfast there and instead had to use a small café up the main road. We had a meal there that night and they told us breakfast was served at 7am. We arrived back to a warmer room and slept all night.

Early the next morning we left our cases in our room to be picked up and taken to Lavacolla. Then we were sat bathed in moonlight, admiring the beautiful stars outside the café at 7am. It was still dark and we had a very simple breakfast – tea and *tostadas* with *mermelada*. Then it was phone torches on as we walked back on to the Camino at about 7.30am.

This time there was no one around and we couldn't see very far, so we took things easy till it got lighter and the sun came up. I will never forget that sky full of stars. It was magical. I could have sat watching it longer but it was usually a bit chilly on a morning so we kept moving.

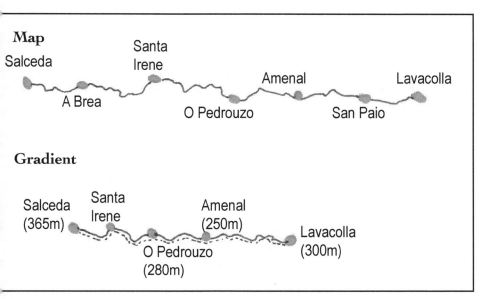

Salceda to Lavacolla
7.5 km or 10.8 miles
'riday 11th October 2019

Today's gradients weren't too bad at all, starting off at 365 m rising to
72 m at Santa Irene then down to 280 m at O Pedrouso, 250 m at Amenal
hen back to 300m at Lavacolla. This walk was lovely in parts because we
aw lots of eucalyptus trees which are really beautiful to look at and to
/alk among. Eucalyptus trees are holy trees for Aboriginal people. The
ood is good for making didgeridoos and the burning of a eucalyptus leaf
urifies and eliminates negative energy. I didn't know this. You might
eed this info for your pub quiz. They contain cineole which is sometimes
nown as eucalyptol and this has been used as an anti bacterial and anti
ungal for hundreds of years. In high concentrations it can be toxic and it
s an excellent insect repellent. I must try this next time I go to Scotland
s Scottish midges are fearsome, I digress, sorry.

We met a French man who was in his 80s who was doing the pilgrimage and camping his way to Santiago. He was on his own and we chatted for ages. He was telling us the story of his false teeth, as you do in a forest of eucalyptus trees. He had apologised when we met him for not having his teeth in. He said they were a bad fit and kept them in his pocket. I felt so sorry for him because he said he would have to wait a long time before he could get them sorted out. He had started the Camino in St Jean Pied de Port and had taken months to get where he was, camping and carrying his tent on his back. But with or without his teeth, he was a lovely man enjoying his adventure alone. We continued walking under the trees and came across a man selling souvenirs so we stopped and bought little presents for our families. The man had a really special stamp, part of which was a real shell which he stuck on to our Credential, the Camino passport. We had to use underpasses to cross the main roads and walked alongside the main Santiago runway – when planes were taking off we could almost wave to the passengers. In the past Lavacolla was the place where pilgrims got washed and cleaned up before entering Santiago. When we arrived in Lavacolla we had to ring the hotel where we were staying which was the Xan Xordo, 900 metres away from the Camino. We were hungry so we told them we were going to have a sandwich at the Ruta Jacobea Hotel cafeteria and we would wait to be picked up there. While we sat there looking weary and windswept with throbbing feet, the entire Santiago de Compostela Football team came out of the very posh dining room, looking every inch the gods of the turf they played on. Some even came across and wished us a *Buen Camino*. Looking at their youthfulness and handsome good looks perked us up and made us realise we were still not too old to admire athletic young men in shorts with tanned brown legs. We didn't however ask for a selfie – that would have been cheeky!

Our hotel tonight, the Pazo Xan Xordo, is out of town and is very traditional with its own chapel and beautiful gardens. I thought the layout was a bit like a convent. I can imagine it being a beautiful venue for a wedding. We had a twin room and our beds had fantastic ornate headboards. The surroundings were beautiful and the food was very good. The company of the other pilgrims was entertaining and we slept really well after talking about how far we had come. We were both so excited about our walk into Santiago and were looking forward to seeing the much talked about Monte de Gozo the next day from which we would be able to see the spires of the cathedral. So tomorrow we have 10 km to walk into Santiago. I can't believe it. In fact I will only believe it when I see the *Compostela* in my hand.

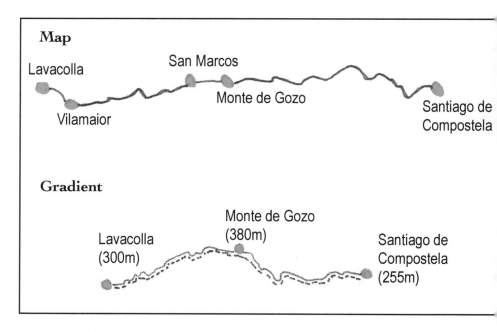

Map

Lavacolla
San Marcos
Monte de Gozo
Vilamaior
Santiago de Compostela

Gradient

Monte de Gozo
(380m)
Lavacolla
(300m)
Santiago de
Compostela
(255m)

Lavacolla to Santiago de Compostela
9.9 km or 6.1 miles
Saturday 12th and Sunday 13th October 2019

We had arranged with the owner to take us back to the Camino route the next morning after breakfast and we were so pleased and excited about the day ahead. Getting out of the car we thanked him and he wished us a *Buen Camino* and drove off. We were so excited. We couldn't wait to start walking and were off with a spring in our step. It was 8.00am, later than usual but we didn't have a long walk today and we knew we could expect real luxury when we checked into the Parador de Santiago de Compostela, in the same square as the Cathedral.

We had decided that we would pamper ourselves when we arrived so had chosen the same hotel where the actors from the film "The Way" had stayed.

Our friends Mikey and Pat from the USA were going to be waiting for us in front of the Cathedral at 7pm that night and that was one date we had no intention of missing. We had met up with them throughout our walk in different places and it would be a grand finish for our Camino.

As we walked along we were buzzing with excitement. We got to the Monte de Gozo and said a quick prayer, took in the view, saw the spires of the cathedral and found it hard to believe that we had come so far. We walked through the outskirts of the city in a state of disbelief. After days of walking we were so happy to be taking everything in, relishing every second. It seemed to take us forever to get there. I had read that as you approach the Cathedral you had to walk through a tunnel to get into the Cathedral area. Me, being me, had read how people said it could get very congested and my claustrophobic fear of tunnels came to the fore. I had actually already walked through the tunnel before I remembered this! For those people out there like me, there is loads of room and plenty of air and you can see daylight all of the time. You are so happy you never notice. Before we knew it Trish and I were gazing up at the Cathedral which unfortunately for us was partly covered because it was being cleaned. It was so amazing to look up at it. We seemed lost for words and very close to tears thinking that we had actually got here. I thought we would have been high fiving or dancing or making a racket. Everybody else was but we were so moved. We had done this. We had struggled at times with aches and pains but had shrugged them off. We stood quiet and close to tears then the adrenalin kicked in and we were laughing and cuddling each other. We had done it! We were going to get our *Compostela*. Who would have thought it? Maybe one person who had been with us every day on that walk – Jim.

Everybody had advised us to go to the Pilgrim Office and get a time to go back and receive our *Compostela* so we did. Our numbers were 739 and 740. They told us it would be sometime that afternoon, so we knew we could happily wander around for a couple of hours and shop if we wanted to. But we had a real treat in store. We still had to check in to our hotel the Parador de Santiago de Compostela. Staying here was he treat we had promised ourselves for completing the Camino. Wow! We walked through three courtyards and had a suite on the second floor. It was sheer luxury. We had an entrance hallway, a lounge and a bedroom with a four poster bed each and a huge bathroom with two wash basins a huge bath and two showers. We dumped our stuff then went downstairs to the bar, still wearing our walking gear, for a plate of chips and a drink, then went back to the office to wait to be called to receive our *Compostela*. When we got there they were calling the 500 numbers. Our hearts were racing and we both seemed a bit on edge – no idea why – but very excited. Finally number 738 was called out and the feeling of knowing we were next was so exciting. I was called in by a very pleasant man who asked me the purpose of my walk. I told him the story of how it was something my husband and I had planned to do but he never got the opportunity because he had died. I also said I had wanted to walk it on his behalf so could I have his name on the *Compostela*? He told me he had the perfect certificate and was very sympathetic. He asked for Jim's full name and handed me the *Compostela*. Jim would have been so proud but he would have laughed seeing his name written in Latin as Iacabum Dryden. I would never have heard the end of it! But it was an amazing feeling to have walked the last part of the Camino. I was so pleased with myself. But how could I not have done it? I had the best reason in the world – love – and I knew how that powerful feeling can make you do anything if you put your mind to it. I never thought that I would be strong enough and how blessed was I doing it with my best friend? We enjoyed every second of that walk. There was

never a cross word. It was a amazing feat. Even when I brok my arm the first question I aske the doctor was could I continu my walk? Getting the *Composte* in Jim's name was the only thin I could think about.

But the walk itself wa amazing. I found peace ju: walking with Trish every day drenched in nature, sunshine mist and, some days, drenche in rain. We had met people wh made you feel humbled an people who were as amazing a the walk.

The Cathedral was amazing and the entrance in Obradoiro Square i the historic quarter of Santiago was teeming with pilgrims of all ages a we walked in. We knew we wouldn't be able to attend the Pilgrims Mas at 7pm so we went straight to see the image of Santiago, St James th apostle. There was a big queue of people and we embraced the imag of the apostle on the High altar and then went down into the crypt t see the actual tomb of the apostle. There are a few other rituals whic: are traditional for dedicated pilgrims, like attending the Pilgrims Mas at noon on arrival in Santiago, placing a hand on the base of the mullio: of the Portico of Glory. I didn't find out till later that if I had hit my hea three times, gently against the statue that represents the Master Mateo might have developed an increased intelligence. I might have to go bacl to do that.

Finally the most amazing part of the mass in the cathedral is the Botafumeiro which is the biggest incense ball or thurible you can imagine. In the Codex Callixtus it is called Turibulum Magnum. I can hear in my mind my lovely Latin teacher, Sister Mackin, saying those words with real feeling and gusto. It is rumoured to weigh 60 kg and is 1.60 metres tall. It hangs in front of the High altar and is not always in use at every Mass. It tends to be swung at the end of Mass on a Sunday –

well that's what the man in the Cathedral told me. I had the privilege of seeing it in action in February 1998 when I attended a language course at the university. The Botafumeiro is carried and swung through the air in the cathedral by eight tiraboleiros, men wearing red robes. It is an amazing sight to witness and I remember just hoping and praying that the ropes and chains were really strong. It seems to start off very slowly but can actually reach a speed of 70 km/h while flying overhead. The last time there was a mishap with a rope was 1937. I did check – how sad am I? I also found it a really moving experience because the smoke rising up to Heaven represents the prayers of all the people. Originally, in former times, it was used to purify the air in the Cathedral when it was filled with pilgrims who had been travelling there for weeks and months in the same clothes. Apparently groups or individuals can make a request for it to be used but have to pay for it and that can cost between 400 and 450 euros. Usually there is a group request for it every day at some point. When we arrived we had missed it and would not be lucky enough to see it on the Sunday because we had planned our trip to Finisterre. Meantime we headed back to our hotel room to smarten ourselves up then go to meet our American friends outside the Cathedral at 7pm. It was so good to see them again and we had a lovely meal. They were really keen to see the hotel so they came back with us for a drink and to soak up the atmosphere.

The next morning Trish and I had to be at a bus stop not too far away because we had booked a trip to Finisterre, Muxia and beyond. We got up early for a breakfast that honestly looked like a banquet. Everything you could think of was laid out. It was so good after living on cereal and *tostadas*. It was the best buffet breakfast I had eaten because there were so many things I enjoyed and I usually eat like a mouse. So I was hopefully a little fat mouse when we left the dining room. It was a real treat. We even managed to make up a sandwich, wrap it in a serviette and take it with us for the bus journey.

Santiago de Compostela to Finisterre

78 miles by bus

Sunday 13th October 2019

Trish and I hurried out of the hotel to the bus stop. Today we were travelling by coach to Cape Finisterre which is a pre-Christian pilgrimage route travelled by people to see where the Sun died and where they believed the world of the dead and the living became closer. Finisterre was called the end of the world by the Romans, until Columbus proved they were wrong. It was a place rich in superstition, legends and pagan rites. It was believed to be a magical place called Ara Solis where there was an altar which was dedicated to the dying Sun. I have to mention that this was also the place where the route marked in the sky by the Milky Way ended. In the past pilgrims would continue their pilgrimage to Finisterre and then continue to Muxia, then they would head for the Sanctuario

de Nuestra Senora de la Barca. The Virgin Mary is said to have landed here in a stone boat along with James the apostle, when he came to convert the people living in this region and who, in later years, was to become St James. She came to encourage him in his preaching mission throughout Galicia.

The large granite stones you see in the sea in front of the Sanctuario, the church, are

said to be the remain
of the sail, the helm
and the actual boa
that Our Lady and S
James sailed in and
are said to posses
special spiritual and
healing powers. This
location has been a
sacred Celtic place
long before St Jame
arrived here.

We all got off the bus in pouring rain to take in the sites, take photo
and then got back into a nice warm bus, dripping water all over the bu
floor. It was so interesting to see that nobody minded. The journey wa
so good and the scenery was stunning as we passed through some very
pretty little villages. Even though the weather was wet when we arrived
in Muxia and it was very grey and misty, we still found the waves were
amazingly scary. This region in Galicia is known as the Costa da Morte o
Coast of Death taking this name because of all the shipwrecks that took
place along this stretch of coastline.

Even on this bus journey we sat talking to a really lovely lady from
Vienna who had walked the entire Camino from St Jean Pied de Port on
her own, with an incurable form of cancer and who wanted to make every
second of the life she had left count. She was so serene and had enough
faith to move mountains. I have to say for me it was a real honour to mee
someone so brave and who was totally at peace with her life. Thinking
about her smiley face and what she said can even now bring tears to my
eyes. The trip to Finisterre was *la guinda del pastel* – the icing on the cake

as we say, for the whole Camino trip. We all said goodbye when we got off the bus and realised our trip was coming to a close. But we still had tonight in our hotel so we made the most of it. We ordered room service after donning our beautifully soft towelling dressing gowns and slippers. I had the most expensive jam and bread I have ever eaten, with a pot of tea and Trish ordered the biggest gin and tonic we both had ever seen. We mulled over our great adventure and realised we were

really excited about going home. We also knew we would be special friends forever. We had shared so much, laughed and cried together, and looked after each other. We were an ace team together and we know we always will be there for each other whatever happens.

Chapter 12
WHAT DID THE CAMINO TEACH ME?

What did I learn? Well, first of all it's still teaching me every single day. It showed me how much I loved and missed my family Tessa, Steven, Rosie and Zoe. How blessed I am to have all my lovely family and true friends in my life – the friends who will suffer alongside you, who will support and help you to achieve something you really want.

It taught me that true love for another person can make you do anything you put your mind to and that they are always going to be with you in spirit and will never ever leave you. They are a part of your heart and soul.

It taught me that whatever happens to you, there are good people out there in the world who will always help you. Like the doctor who rang my hotel to tell them I had left a bag of ice melting on a unit in the hotel room; like the man in the hospital who rang for a taxi for us at 3am when our phones had died then escorted us outside and told the taxi driver to take care of us.

It taught me that true friendship is like gold, to be valued. I don't know if I could have done the Camino without Trish. Even she went into it with some trepidation but we coped. We have been friends since we were 5 years old and we had great fun discovering that we are still and that we make a brilliant team.

It taught me that friendship is a gift in itself. A real friendship stays the same no matter how old you are, how far away you live and how many years go by and I realised how much I should value my friends.

It taught me how much I love all of my family and how much I was looking forward to coming home to them. Every one of them had helped and encouraged me to do the Camino. I knew that I would try hard not to be sad when I got home because Trish and I both knew Jim was with us on that walk and I really believe he will stay in my heart and be there when I need him, whatever happens to me in life.

It taught me that you are never too old to make new friends and the friends you make on the Camino are people you are meant to meet. You meet them for one reason or another out of the hundreds of people you pass every day and there is always something special about them. They will have something to say that will help you along your own journey hrough life. You talk to these people you meet and get an insight into heir lives and you realise that everyone has something to cope with, to ry to come to terms with and accept as best they can.

It taught me to treasure all the good people and the good positive hings I have in my own life and enjoy what I have. It taught me I am blessed in what I have had, what I still have and it taught me that God s always with you and so are the people you have loved in life and lost. They are not lost – they walk beside you through the good and the bad imes, which brings me to my surprising conclusion. It taught me that I don't just like walking, I actually love walking. It's a gift we should never ake for granted. Walking calmed me, the scenery around me made me feel uplifted, setting off in starlight with the red glow of the sun coming up was amazing. Being a part of this was so good and it happens every day and it's free to be appreciated along with the chatter of the birds. I felt at one with the world I was walking in. I knew Jim was part of this and I felt energised, positive and free of sadness because everything was buzzing with life and we were at one with this wonderful world we never knew existed. Now I understand what John Muir meant when he said "In every walk with nature, one receives far more than he seeks." I felt nature healing my heart every day on the Camino and I realised if you really want to do something, don't think of excuses, take the chance, live your life and just do it.

I know that there will be many other things that I learned from the Camino and I know I will keep coming across them in the future.

Finally a letter to Jim:

Hi Jim,

I can't believe it, Trish and I did the Camino but you knew all along we would didn't you? No doubts at all and on the walk to Santiago I discovered that I loved seeing my robin every single day. I loved seeing nature at its finest. I loved walking through beautiful trees that you would have known the names of. I loved meeting the lovely people who walked into our lives for different reasons, I loved walking in the rain with waterproofs on and feeling the water running down my face. It made me feel alive, it renewed and refreshed my mind and my soul. I loved the sense of achievement I felt looking up at the Cathedral knowing how love can make you do things you think are impossible. I know I will always love you and now I know that your love has given me wings to fly if I want to. I can do things on my own if I want to, I know that if bad things happen there are always good people who are around to help you. Just one more thing Jim Dryden. I know I will love you forever just like you said, "Forever mind Lynnie."

Love Lynn xx

WHERE WE STAYED ON THE CAMINO

First of all, I would like to thank Hays Travel for booking all our trains and flights. Everything ran smoothly, just the way we wanted. I also have to say that we booked our trip and our accommodation on the Camino through the tour company Santiago Ways. We had asked for nice, comfortable places to stay and their choices did not disappoint. Everything they planned for us was perfect. So a big thank you. We would love to come back and booking with Santiago Ways will give us total peace of mind. Thank you for making a very important trip absolutely perfect. If you are thinking of planning your own trip I can recommend any of these hotels where we were happy to stay.

Sarria

The Hotel Mar de Plata,

Rúa de los Formigueiros, 5,

27600 Sarria,

Lugo, Spain

Tel +34 982 53 07 24

Ferreiros

Albergue – Restaurante Casa Cruceiro de Ferreiros, 2,

Ferreiros, Spain

Tel +34 639 02 00 64

Portomarin

Vistalegre Hotel

Travesia de Compostela, No 29

27170 Portomarin,

Lugo, Spain

Tel +34982545076

Ventas de Narón

Albergue O Cruceiro, Ventas de Narón, 6,

27212 Lugo, Spain

Tel +34 658 06 49 17

Palas de Rei

Albergue y Pensión San Marcos,

Travesia da Igrexa, s/n,

27200 Palas de Rei,

Lugo, Spain

Hotel Mica.

Calle Cruceiro No12,

27200 Palas de Rei,

Lugo, Spain

Tel +34 982 17 93 11

Melide

Pousada Chiquitin

Calle de San Antonio, 18

15800 Melide,

A Coruña, Spain

Tel +34 981 81 53 33

Arzúa

Casa Branderiz
Calle Dombodan, s/n,
15819 Arzúa,
A Coruña, Spain
Tel + 34 609 572 817

Salceda

Pension Albergue Alborada
Carretera Nacional 547, Km.27.48,
15824 O Pino,
A Coruña, Spain
Tel + 34 620 15 12 09

Lavacolla

Pazo Xan Xordo, 6
15820 Lavacolla,
A Coruña, Spain
Tel + 34 981 88 82 59

Santiago De Compostela

Parador De Santiago De Compostela
Prazo do Obradoiro, 1,
15704 Santiago de Compostela,
A Coruña Spain
Tel +34 981 582 200

NOTES ON THE HAND-DRAWN MAPS

I drew these maps by hand only so that you know which towns and villages you will be walking through. On the maps, I have marked the towns we passed through. Where each map finishes is where we stayed. We booked all of our trip through Santiago Ways and every bit of their service was brilliant, including their maps. My own maps are not drawn to scale and the heights I have put in on the gradients, are what I could find on Google and they seemed to vary depending on where I looked. Basically, I put the gradients in only so you can look at them just before you have your breakfast (definitely not the night before, after a hard day's walking) and this will help you to calculate how many extra cornflakes you will need to get up those hills.

It's also nice to know if you will have spectacular views from a great height; then you can have your camera or phone handy. What I should have put on my maps as well are the little cafés where you can get snacks and meals. But, believe me, there are plenty along all of this part of the Camino and you will be spoilt for choice. My other worry was being able to find a loo. Again it's nothing to worry yourself about as the café owners are happy for you to use their loos, no problem. There are also plenty of trees you can hide behind (just glance around before you get settled – you don't want to moon everyone as they walk by like some unfortunate person we passed). Everyone you meet on the walk goes out of their way to help you in any way they can. Always just ask, people are good.

Sarria to Ferreiros

A pleasant walk taking in the Camino scenery and everything that's part of it, a great start.

Ferreiros to Portomarin

Beautiful scenery, a choice of routes as well. Take the easier route if you dislike clambering down a dry waterfall. Look at the steps up into Portomarin and don't think, "Just do it". It's a beautiful place and well worth the effort.

Portomarin to Ventas de Narón

A walk through lots of pine trees and forested areas into open fields and alongside the main road at times. The Albergue in Ventas de Narón next to the tiny chapel is a friendly place to stay and very popular for food and drink.

Ventas de Narón to Palas de Rei

An undulating walk but plenty of views to admire. Look out for the stone bollards outside the Town Hall in Concello Square in Palas de Rei. They move and trip unsuspecting pilgrims up, breaking their arm!

Palas de Rei to Melide

Nothing too hard today. Tie your laces and enjoy the walk. You're heading into octopus territory.

Melide to Arzúa

A bit up and down today and you will see eucalyptus trees which I think are lovely. There are also oak and pine trees and lots of other trees I don't know the names of. The walk into Arzúa is much easier when it's not raining and windy and is a bit long, but there is a café at the top, I promise.

Arzúa to Salceda

Another undulating walk today through trees and alongside the main road at times as you approach Salceda.

Salceda to Lavacolla

Walking is a bit up and down, then you walk past the end of the runway of Santiago Airport. If a plane takes off you can wave to the pilot and passengers – really.

Lavacolla to Santiago

Who cares what today's walk is like. If it was over hot coals would it bother you? No way! Enjoy every step you take towards your goal. Views from Monte do Gozo (The hill of Joy) are brilliant, not to mention the mounting anticipation you feel as you are walking through the streets into Santiago searching for the Cathedral in the Praza do Obradoiro. What a feeling!

Remember no looking at the gradients till the morning you are walking. If you don't like them, just grit your teeth, tie your laces, pick up your backpack and put one foot in front of the other. You will do it and will feel so proud. Well done!

Useful Spanish Phrases

It's amazing how many people speak English in Galicia but you will come across areas where you might need a bit of help. Sometimes you might not know how to ask the question but if you know the word of whatever it is you need just say it with the question in your tone of voice, followed by please in Spanish *"¿por favor?"* and people will understand. If you need help there are usually people around you who can speak on your behalf.

General phrases

Yes = Si

No = No

Hello = ¡Hola!

Goodbye = ¡Adiós!

Please = Por favor

Thank you (very much) = (Muchas) gracias

Good morning = Buenos dias

Good afternoon = Buenos tardes

Good evening = Buenas noches

Excuse me = ¡Perdón!

Sorry = ¡Lo siento!

Do you speak English? = ¿Habla inglés?

I don't speak Spanish = No hablo español

I don't understand = No entiendo

I understand = Entiendo

Could you speak more slowly please? = ¿Podria hablar más despacio por favor?

What does this mean? = ¿Que significa esto?

Asking for directions

Where is ...? = ¿Dónde está ...?

Where is the lift please? = ¿Dónde está el ascensor por favor?

Where is the cathedral/the shopping area, please? = ¿Dónde está la cathedral / la zona de tiendas, por favor?

Where are the toilets please? = ¿Dónde están los servicios, por favor?

Is there ...? = ¿Hay...?

Near = cerca

Next to = al lado de

Opposite = enfrente

There = allí

On the right = a la derecha

On the left = a la izquierda

Can you tell me how to get to...? = ¿Puede indicarme cómo ir a...?

In a hotel

I have a reservation. My name is... = Tengo una reserva. Me llamo...

Do you have any rooms? = ¿Tienen habitaciones libres?

The room is cold = La habitación es frio.

Hot = caliente

Cold = frio

Quiet = silencioso

Noisy = ruidoso

Quick = rápido

Ordering food

Do you have a set menu? = ¿Tienen un menú del día?

Do you have vegetarian food? = ¿Tienen comidas vegetarianas?

How much is that? = ¿Cuánto es?

Can I have the bill please? = ¿La cuenta por favor?

I am allergic to nuts. = Soy alérgico a las nueces.

I am allergic to penicillin. = Soy alérgico a la penicilina. (masculine)
Soy alérgica a la penicilina. (feminine)

I'd like ... = Quiero...

Food

Soup = sopa
A portion of chips = una porción de patatas fritas
Vegetables = verduras
A hamburger = una hamburguesa
An omelette = una tortilla
Chicken = pollo
Ham = jamon
Sausages = salchichas
Cheese = queso
Spicy sausage = chorizo
Rice = arroz
Salad = ensalada
A cheese sandwich = un bocadillo de queso
Bread = pan
Butter = mantequilla
Jam = mermelada
An ice-cream = un helado
      strawberry = de fresa
      chocolate = de chocolate
      vanilla = de vanilla

Drinks

A tea = un té
A coffee = un café
      black = solo

with milk = con leche

A hot chocolate = un chocolate

A mineral water = un agua mineral

A lemonade = una limonada

A wine = un vino

      red = tinto

      white = blanco

A beer = una cerveza

Medical problems

Where is there a doctor who speaks English? = ¿Dónde hay un médico que hable inglés?

You need to go to hospital. = Tienes que ir al hospital.

My arm hurts here. = Mi brazo me duele aquí.

My foot hurts. = Me duele el pie.

My stomach hurts. = Me duele el estómago.

My leg hurts. = Me duele la pierna.

My head hurts. = Me duele la cabeza

I have = tengo

You can use Tengo + dolor de + the body part:

I have a headache. = Tengo dolor de cabeza

Back = espalda

Ears = oidos

I think you will manage with the words I have written and remember look up the name of what you want then just ask somebody and follow the word with *Por favor.* For example: *¿Los servicios, por favor?*

You will find most people you meet will speak English but if they don't please try and you will feel pleased with yourself. They will like you for rying as well. If in doubt just point to what you want and say *Qué es esto, por favor?* The more you try, the more chuffed you will be with yourself.

SOURCES OF INSPIRATION AND INFORMATION

I started to read books about the Camino after I had watched the film *The Way* at the cinema a good few years ago when it first came out in November 2010. I was fascinated by the Camino and the experiences of the people who had written books about it. I will list all the books I read, but this book was written every night when we had walked all day on our Camino in 2019. Trish my friend used to fall asleep before our evening meal and I used that time to make my notes about what had happened each day and what we had seen. My notebook was tiny and easily fitted in my backpack. I had read so much about the places we visited in other books. It was amazing how I had been able to imagine what they were like and at other times how different they were in my imagination. I had seen some of the places in photographs, but not all. I have to say all the places we walked through and stayed at were lovely and all the people we met on our journey were amazing

A big thank you to all of these authors who I read so avidly. You all inspired me in some way and made me think I could do it. It took me nine years and a catastrophic change in my life to make the decision to go and see what the Camino could do for a broken heart. What it did for me I can't really put into words except that I know it changed me for the good and made me a better person. It gave me strength to cope with every day and helped me see a more positive side to life and to see positivity in the people around me. It made me appreciate everyone in my life who stood beside me – encouraging me to keep chasing a life that makes me happy. I know I didn't walk the whole Camino but that was never my plan. I loved reading your books and you gave me the confidence to walk my own Camino. I also never thought that I would be able or talented enough to write my own book about what it was like

o for other people like me, take that leap of faith and go and check it
ut.

The Camino by Shirley MacLaine
Call of the Camino by Robert Mullen
The Best Way El Camino de Santiago by Bill Walker "Skywalker"
Off the road A Modern Day Walk Down the Pilgrims Route into
Spain by Jack Hitt
In Movement there is Peace by Elaine Orabona Foster and Joseph
Wilbred Foster 111.
Buen Camino ! by Natasha and Peter Murtagh
A Way, the Story of a Long Walk by Jenna Smith
I'm off then by Hape Kerkeling
Grandma's on the Camino by Mary O'Hara Wyman
To Walk Far, Carry Less by Jean- Christie Ashmore
The Only way is West by Kevin Hand BBC
Field of Stars. A Story of the road to Santiago by Susie Tarver
Walk In a Relaxed Manner. Life lessons on the Camino by Joyce
Rupp
Camino Chronicle Walking to Santiago by Susan Alcorn
The Way, My Way by Bill Bennet
Camino de Santiago in 20 days by Randall St. Germain
Spanish Steps. Travels with my Donkey by Tim Moore
Camino, Laughter and Tears along Spain's 500mile Camino de
Santiago by John H Clark 111.
Walking the Camino de Santiago by Bethan Davies and Ben Cole
Fisterra, Muxia Experience by Mike Day
A Pilgrims Guide to the Camino de Santiago by John Brierley (An
amazing book)

I would also like to say a big thank you to Santiago Ways who booked our holiday and provided us with an excellent information pack about the Camino they had planned for us. The service you provided was first class, thank you. Nothing was too much trouble for you and I would recommend you for people like us who just want to walk and know that everything else is taken care of. *¡Muchas gracias!*

The Camino I have written about is a result of reading everything I could about each place I would be visiting in the all the books, guides and leaflets I could find and, of course, information I looked up on Google and hints and tips I picked up in the conversations I had with my friends and acquaintances who I talked to after they had completed the Camino. Going out there and being a part of the Camino for two weeks I thought I had prepared myself well for each place we visited. But until you see the places with your own eyes and feel the magic in your heart at the same time, all they seem to be are interesting facts which become so special to you when you are there. You can read about the Camino and feel excited about it, but walking it in your own way gladdens your heart and leaves you with a feeling of happiness and wonder. It's out there waiting, so go and walk it.

Milton Keynes UK
Ingram Content Group UK Ltd.
UKHW021816130923
428619UK00009B/375